WHAT PEO

MW00989699

PAGAN PORTALS – THE AWEN ALONE

Joanna's language is delightful, it lights up the heart with joy, enchanting you...
Elen Sentier, author of *Shaman Pathways: Elen of the Ways*

This is one of the best 'core' texts on Druidry that I have had the pleasure of reading. Small but perfectly formed, Joanna paints a succinct, yet broad picture of Druidry past and present – not just the historic foundations, but also the lived practices of contemporary Druids. Given the diversity of the latter, she acts as an excellent guide and teacher through the potentially murky woods, encouraging personal exploration to find the inspiration that is the heart of Druidry. Heartily recommended.
Cat Treadwell, author *of A Druid's Tale* and *Facing the Darkness*

This little book lays out about as idealistic a vision of Druidism as one can hope for. According to tradition, the ancient Druids spent at least twenty years in study before claiming that title, and there are many excellent books and teachers in the world who can provide the Druid initiate with the knowledge of the ancient laws and teachings. But this is not a book about Celtic scholarship or the historical Celts; rather it is a guide to how to BE a modern Druid in the world today. The author teaches aspiring Druids to be ecologically conscious, wise persons who act with reverence towards all life, because after all we are all related; plants, trees, animals, people, and spiritual beings. The book takes us into our inner wild places, and to the outer wilderness of our forests, parks and backyards, to honour the spirits and ancestors of the land, the spirits of our own blood ancestors, and the spirits of the ancestors of the future who will walk the same path (if we are so lucky). Joanna van der Hoeven reminds us that Druidism is our own indigenous European native Earth Religion. How much healthier would the Earth be today if we had retained our ancient reverence for the sacred Land and its creatures?

Ellen Evert Hopman, author of *A Druid's Herbal of Sacred Tree Medicine, Priestess of the Forest, The Druid Isle, Priestess of the Fire Temple*, and other volumes. www.elleneverthopman.com

Becoming Druid is a commitment to a lifelong and complex journey. This book offers a down-to-earth guide to setting out. It is enthusiastic, based in good practice, and allows the reader to start with sound and gentle steps. I heartily recommend it.

Graeme K Talboys, author of *Way of the Druid: Rebirth of an Ancient Religion* and *The Druid Way Made Easy*

Druidry can seem like an innately gregarious path, which makes things difficult for the person called, or obliged, to work alone. This is an excellent introduction to working as a solitary Druid, establishing solitary Druidry as an equally valid approach to the more familiar, communal methods. In practice, even the most convivial Druid will not be with their Grove every day, and we can all benefit from considering how we express our Druidry privately.

Nimue Brown, author of *Druidry and Meditation*, and *Druidry and the Ancestors*

Pagan Portals
The Awen Alone

Walking the Path of the Solitary Druid

Pagan Portals
The Awen Alone

Walking the Path of the Solitary Druid

Joanna van der Hoeven

Winchester, UK
Washington, USA

First published by Moon Books, 2014
Moon Books is an imprint of John Hunt Publishing Ltd., Laurel House, Station Approach,
Alresford, Hants, SO24 9JH, UK
office1@jhpbooks.net
www.johnhuntpublishing.com
www.moon-books.net

For distributor details and how to order please visit the 'Ordering' section on our website.

Text copyright: Joanna van der Hoeven 2014

ISBN: 978 1 78279 547 6

A CIP catalogue record for this book is available from the British Library.

Design: Lee Nash

Printed and bound by CPI Group (UK) Ltd, Croydon, CR0 4YY

We operate a distinctive and ethical publishing philosophy in all
areas of our business, from our global network of authors to
production and worldwide distribution.

CONTENTS

This book is dedicated to those who have decided to walk the forest path alone.
May we walk our paths with honour.

Special thanks to my husband, Trevor. I love you.

Thank you to Emily from *Photography by Emily Fae* for the cover photo art:
www.photographybyemilyfae.com

Introduction

The alarm clock goes off; Aerosmith are playing on Planet Rock. There is a small white cat lying between me and my husband, her little head resting on my pillow. A spotted grey cat is curled up against the small of my back, sharing in the warmth. My husband gets up, showers and comes back to kiss me goodbye. I sigh, stretch, and slowly extricate myself from the sleeping, furry softness to greet the day.

Standing by the top landing window, overlooking my back garden and the horse paddocks beyond that, down the valley towards the little nature sanctuary, my eyes come back full circle to see the sun, rising on the horizon. I let its light wash over me – sunny mornings have been few and far between, and with eyes closed I drink it in. "Hail to the Day, and Day's Sons, farewell to Night and her Daughters. With loving eyes look upon us here, and grant peace to those living here. Hail to the Gods, hail to the Goddesses, hail to the mighty fecund Earth. Eloquence and native wit bestow upon us here, and healing hands while we live." I smile and let the words of my prayer seep into my soul. Another deep breath, and so the day begins.

Heading downstairs, I get food ready for the cats, and boil the kettle for my tea. The cats slowly make their way downstairs to breakfast. After getting my lunch ready, I prepare my own breakfast, and sit down at the table with a cup of nettle tea, the young nettles picked from my garden the day before. "I give my thanks for this food I am about to eat. To the spirits of land, sea and sky, know that you are honoured."

After breaking my fast I head back upstairs to get ready for work. Using toiletries that are from ethical companies, I grumble once again at the price of these organic, non-animal tested cosmetics, but then I catch myself – it is better than the alternative, and I am saving money in other areas of my life, such as in my vow not to buy any new clothing for a year. I can afford it.

After dressing, I say goodbye to the cats and head out of the door to drive to work. I give thanks that I am blessed in that I both live and work in the countryside. On the drive to work, I like to listen to music, to hear the inspiration of others, yet I remain focused on my driving – winding slowly down country lanes, watching out for rabbits, hares, deer and the occasional oncoming tractor around the next blind bend. The fields have been ploughed and seeded, the fabric canopies protecting those crops susceptible to late frosts. The white blankets over the brown, sandy soil glisten over the softly rolling hills, looking like shining lakes in the distance. I pray for a good crop this year, as last year's winter was too dry and the summer too wet. They are already three to four weeks behind schedule this year, with the prolonged winter weather.

At work, it is a busy time, but I try to stay focused, remaining in the here and now as much as I can, giving every task the same attention. At one point, a colleague does not help me when I ask for it – moving heavy boxes to another location – and I feel anger rising within me. I then breathe deeply, and a colleague from another department offers to help, for which I am thankful. We move the boxes, and I release the anger – I cannot expect people to behave the way that I think they should. I can only lead by example, and not let it affect me so.

The day is tiring, and when home time comes I am thankful. Physically and mentally tired, I walk back to my car, taking the time to decompress. Where I work is one of the most beautiful spots in the county, along the river with the reed beds swaying in the wind, the large skies opening out before me. I listen to the birds, breathe in the salt marsh air, and smile.

The drive home is in silence. I open the car window slightly to feel the breeze against my skin and to smell the emerging spring scents. I am wholly focused on driving, feeling the road through the tyres and the steering wheel, the sand that is being washed onto the roads due to lack of hedgerows and adequate space between fields and roadside.

I pull into the driveway of my home and turn off the car engine, giving thanks once again. Walking to my front door I notice the crocuses, tulips, daffodils and primroses all out at the same time in this late spring weather, stretching towards the late afternoon sun. I too am going to stretch towards it. I walk into the porch and, coming through the front door, touch the doorframe, whispering a soft prayer to my goddess, Nemetona; Lady of Sanctuary.

After greeting my cats and feeding them, my growling stomach demands attention and I eat, giving thanks once again to the spirits of land, sea and sky. My husband comes home, and I smile at the welcome, comfort and love that I am blessed with.

After dinner I wrap up and head out into the backyard, walking the perimeter, singing songs of love and gratitude to the spirits of the land. Grape hyacinths are starting to come through, alongside the daffodils, crocuses and tulips. The irises are starting to recover and grow back after being munched by the muntjac deer early in the spring, as are the sisyrinchium tipped with black edges along the frostbitten leaves. The apple trees have little buds on them, and the first frog spawn is in the pond. I whisper words of welcome to the new little lives, hoping that the pond will not freeze again. I know the newts are secretly lying within the mud and leaves at the bottom of the pond, and wonder when they will emerge this year.

The beech tree calls, and I go to sit under its majestic canopy, still bare but far-reaching. The tree is about 80 years old, and I feel a kinship to it at this point in my life – it feels like a middle-aged tree, strong and comfortable within its skin. I feel the edges of my nemeton touching that of the tree, noting where they meet and where they blend. We are still getting to know each other, the tree and I, and little moments like these are splendid.

I sit on the mossy ground by my little altar under the beech tree. Placing my hands upon the ground, I feel the earth slowly stirring from the long winter slumber. I simply sit, meditating upon being present, feeling the warming ground, hearing the children at play on the football pitches two fields over, the neighbours saying goodbye to someone. The blackbirds are singing and fighting over territory, and a little wren is looking for tasty morsels among the leaf mould. The watery sun hangs low in the sky, the warmth fading fast as night approaches.

After my meditation, I head inside for a hot bath. Sliding into the warm water I sigh with pleasure; the scents of chamomile and the soft oats feeding my skin and my senses. I honour the spirit of water and think of where my water comes from, honouring that source as well, giving thanks for the luxury of clean, hot water.

The sun is setting as I dry off, and once again I stand by my window on the top landing, looking out over the little bit of land that I am getting to know after a few years of having lived here. The light is fading, and the only birds about are the blackbirds with their large dark eyes, singing in the dusk. The owls and their young will soon be hooting in the ash trees. Soon the cuckoo will arrive, and the crickets will be singing. I long for summer, then catch myself – be present. I take a deep breath and ground myself, centring on the here and now. "Farewell to the Day, and Day's Sons, hail to Night and her Daughters. With loving eyes, look upon us here, and grant peace to those living here. Hail to the Gods, hail to the Goddesses, hail to the mighty fecund Earth. Eloquence and native wit bestow upon us here, and healing hands while we live."

With pleasure I crawl into bed, cats coming to join me, and later my husband. I read for a bit, and then when my eyes are too tired, I close the book and enter the world of dreams, thankful for all that I have.

Druidry is a wonderful, spiritually fulfilling life path. This life path can be shared with others, joining Druid Orders and Groves, meeting up at festivals and certain moon phases, sharing inspiration and conversation, joy and laughter. However, this can also be a life path for those who wish to journey on their own, free from social convention and restrictions, finding wonder in the withdrawal, moving away from humanity in order to better know the world at large. This book is for those who feel called to Druidry and wish to walk alone, for however long a time. It is about exploration and connection with the natural world, and finding our place within it. We will cover the basics of Druidry, and discuss how it can be applied to everyday life, enriching it with a sense of beauty, magic and mystery. As part of the Pagan Portals series, this book is only a brief introduction to the subject, and you will find there is much more to learn should you so desire.

This book is not a condemnation of Druid Orders, Groves, societies or groups. In fact, I have been and still am a member of certain groups, but prefer to follow a more solitary path, away from the distraction and noise of the everyday and finding out where I personally can be of use in the world. There is great inspiration in getting together with a group of like-minded people, sharing ideas and stories. Knowing that there are others out there may make you feel a little less alone in the world.

Through the magic that is Druidry, on the solitary path we come to realise that we are never alone in the world, and through our connection to the natural environment we see that ideas of separation are illusion. We aim to immerse ourselves in the present moment, in the present environment, in order to share in the blessing that is the cycle of life. Throughout the ages, people have withdrawn from the world in order to connect more fully with it. This book is for those people who feel a calling to seek their own path, to use their wit, intelligence, compassion and honour to create their own tradition within Druidry. This is sometimes referred to as "Hedge Druidry", much as the tradition of "Hedge Witchcraft" has become more and more popular.

There are some brilliant Druid Orders and Groves, networks and societies. I have listed some of these at the end of this book, if at any stage you feel the call to work with others, to embrace a communal ethos, to follow a path that many others have followed before or to find the shared language of a tribe.

For those who wish to take the solitary path, finding their own feet in the stillness and silence of the deep woods, welcome.

Section One

Basics of Druidry

Here we will look at the basic tenets of Druidry that are held in common, as well as a brief history and a look at the eight Druid festivals. This is to provide a foundation for the solitary Druid's spiritual practice, grounded in the essentials.

Chapter One

A Brief History of the Druids

For anyone beginning on the Druid path, an understanding of the known history of Druidry is essential. In order to better understand a religion or philosophy, one has to know the historical and cultural contexts from which it derived. Therefore, I present here a very short history of the Druids – for more information, please see the bibliography and suggested reading section at the end of this book.

Who Were the Celts?

To look at Druid History we must look to the history of the Celts, who they were and where they came from. There is a growing theory that the Celts had Indo-European roots dating back to around 4000 BCE, and migrated across Europe to finally settle in France, Britain and Ireland. The large Celtic migration theory holds that the Celts, after arriving in Britain, came across the native British tribes, either warring with the native tribes or marrying into them. There is another theory, however, that proposes the native tribes grew into bigger and more socially complex societies, which some Continental Celts settled into, and from which the Celtic cultural and religious ideas spread into Europe rather than the other way around. This theory would hold that Druidry is the native religion of Britain. Both theories are interesting and as yet remain to be 100% proven, however, the leaning is still towards larger migrations with waves of invasions into Britain.

It is difficult to interpret Druid history, as indeed like most history accounts, the story was written usually by the winners or by those hostile to the Celts in various forms. The ancient Celtic peoples followed an oral tradition, and as such there are no written records available in their own voice. Classical sources have written about the Celts, describing them as barbaric, or if feeling more generous, noble savages. They write of a hierarchy based upon the tribe's standing in war – essentially the strongest arm ruled the tribe and/or many other tribes. They also describe women warriors as equally fierce as their male counterparts.

The Druids are commonly believed to the priestly caste of the Celts, whose service was to the Gods and to their people. The perception is that they held considerable sway in the sociological foundations of Celtic life, being the law-makers and king-makers. The Druids and indeed the Celts abided largely by the concept of giving their word – once given it was exceedingly distasteful to rescind. This is comparable to the importance of reputation – what was said of a person was highly regarded in Celtic society. A person's reputation was linked to their standing in society, where being strong, generous, brave, wise and just was the ideal.

In Ireland, there was already an established code of living, the rudiments of Brehon Law. This formed the basis of society and of a native legal system that had developed before the arrival of Christianity (said legal system being later abolished in the 17th century thanks to Cromwell). Honour was all-important to Brehon Law – your code of conduct was determined by it, and deviance from the law resulted in dishonour to clan, tribe and the self. It contained the moral power of the people who followed it. Indeed, the sustainability and durability of Brehon Law is considerable, existing in Ireland since before the Common Era and surviving to see the reign of Queen Elizabeth I.

Brehon law consisted of many aspects of everyday life, including care and responsibility to one's tribe or community. Hospitals had already been running when Christianity arrived in Ireland. A form of welfare for those in need had been established. Medical practitioners had strict codes of conduct to follow. Honour prices had to be paid for transgressions against the law, such as a blood price for killing. The laws centred around the concepts of personal responsibility, the upholding of truth, service and simple common sense.

Classical and Other Sources

In 58 to 51 BCE, Julius Caesar led the Roman armies in the Gallic wars, conquering many Celtic kingdoms and chiefdoms in Gaul. Subsequently, the new rulers saw the threat that the Druid priest caste held, and took measures to remove them utterly from society. Emperor Tiberius banned Druidry, as well as those who read auguries and those who were healers (according to Pliny the Elder). Later accounts from other philosophers and academics relate to the law passed by Emperor Claudius that banned the once accepted form of incorporating many gods of differing pantheons in Roman culture, saying that one could not be a citizen of Rome and a Druid at the same time.

Caesar claimed in his texts that the Druids were one of two highly regarded classes in Celtic society, the other being equites, or horsemen. He writes that the Druids were the power behind kings, and acted as judges to all. Caesar also writes of the Druid belief in reincarnation, and their proficiency in astronomy, biology and theology. He also points out human sacrifice within the Druid rites, making much of the barbarism (ironic, considering his own culture's gladiatorial arenas). It must be said that modern historians widely regard Caesar's accounts as biased, greatly exaggerated and incredibly inaccurate, and that they were written in justification of a Celtic conquest.

Later sources mention Druids after the Christianisation of Britain and Ireland, written mostly by Christian monks – again hostile to the pagan Celts. The knowledge of Celtic culture and society by Christian monks is also questionable. However, Druidry did not die out completely with the coming of the Christians. There was simply a merging of the two in many areas, an adoption of sacred times and places and placing Christian iconography and theology over the top of the earthier pagan underlayers. Druid colleges that existed in Ireland and Britain transformed into Bardic colleges and were said to have existed up until the 17th century, and even possibly later. There is even the hypothesis that many Bardic colleges simply became Christian monasteries.

These Bardic colleges endeavoured to retain and preserve poetry, history, mythology and indeed genealogy as well as some of the "magical" practices. However, in the early 17th century the Flight of the Earls saw patronage of Bardic colleges fade, and eventually dissipate. There is a theory that "hedge schools" were created by those who carried the teaching in the forms of music and poetry as wandering minstrels, and the word "bard" was often used to describe this caste.

The Druid Revival

The 18th century saw the birth of the Druid Revival, with the writings of John Aubrey, John Toland and William Stukeley becoming popular. Aubrey's theories on, and surveys of, Stonehenge and Avebury awakened a romantic longing of (incorrectly) connecting the sites with the ancient Druids. Toland was inspired by Aubrey and continued using Aubrey's theories as a platform. Stukeley too was interested in the archaeology of Avebury and Stonehenge. However, he had the bad timing of arriving a little too late, for the fashion of liking all things ancient and Druid had begun to change. He later became a clergyman, incorporating ideas of Druidic groves of trees and megaliths into his own personal life, and vicarage gardens!

Towards the latter end of the 18th century a second revival was started in 1781 with Henry Hurle founding the Ancient Order of Druids in a London tavern. They incorporated Masonic ideas into their interpretation of Druidry, some of which were good, such as charitable work and community support, others absurd, such as gender-exclusive male gatherings filled with patriarchal ideas.

Edward Williams, otherwise known as Iolo Morganwg, wrote many scripts that he claimed were founded on ancient Druidry, but which, in fact, had been mostly (if not entirely) forged by the man himself. While beautiful and inspiring, it was only 150 years after his death that the forgeries were revealed.

The Celtic Twilight emerged in the late half of the 19th century with the poetic writings of Yeats leading the forefront. This brought forth a renewed interest in the study of all things Celtic, with translations of old texts and re-telling of Celtic myths becoming popular through the works of people such as Lady Gregory, Alfred Nutt and John Rhys among others.

Druidry in the 20th century was further established by the likes of Ross Nichols and Lewis Spence, and interest spread into America in the early 1960s. Druidry held for some an equally attractive mystical path to follow that differed from the growing interest in all things Eastern, such as Buddhism. From the 1980s onwards, prolific Druids such as Philip Carr-Gomm, Philip Shallcrass, and Emma Restall Orr made Druidry more accessible to everyone, bringing it up to date and begetting the tide of information and books that is now becoming more and more abundant on the subject of Druidry all over the globe.

Chapter Two

What is Druidry?

So, what is Druidry?

Druidry is the "native" spiritual tradition of Britain, Ireland and parts of Europe, and has now become a path followed by people from all over the globe. As an ancient pagan tradition, it reinforces a relationship between people and the land.

Druidry is often likened to a philosophy – it is indeed a way of life that does not require a belief in any external deity (though many Druids do see it as a religion, with their own deities). Druidry seeks to strengthen the bonds of our relationship with the natural world, gaining inspiration and wisdom from studying the patterns that nature is constantly unfolding around us and using that as inspiration for a more holistic way of life. At its very core, Druidry holds a reverence for nature. It is about attuning to the cycles of nature that we often find ourselves distanced from in this modern world, and finding the wisdom of the oak (from the Indo European word *dru*, meaning oak, and *wid*, meaning wisdom – hence, "Druid").

The Druid takes inspiration from the natural world around her – she delights in a cold winter's morning as she watches foxes scamper and chase each other across a field newly covered with snow. She feels the heat and passion as she hears the calls of the rutting deer in the cold autumn months. She finds pure joy in the flight of the butterfly searching for food and warmth in the summer sunshine. She finds the thrill of the hunt as she watches a cat stalking its prey. She takes wing with the hawk as it soars across a cloudy sky, finding thermals in ever increasing spirals that reflect the spirals of life. She hears the songs of humanity thrumming through the city centre, honouring the spirits of human nature.

Being a Druid is about taking responsibility for one's actions, as well as for one's environment. No longer can one be ignorant about either – it is waking up and making a commitment to understand, to the best of our abilities, everything that we do and say. It is learning about the behavioural patterns in our own selves as well as in those that share our environment. It is learning from the cycles of nature, the seasons, the tides and times of life. It is knowing when to break free, when to retreat, when to shout aloud and when to keep quiet.

Being a Druid is about making life choices in everything – from vigilant recycling to knowing where our tap water comes from. It is about making a relationship with everything, from the food we eat to the badgers that have lost their homes due to the new housing development. It is a huge sacrifice – giving up ignorance and opening our eyes to the world, seeing what we can do to make it a better place.

We may wear robes, we may wear wellies – but we are still Druids. We may not call down lightning to smite our foes, but we fight in subtler ways to protect those of the natural world that humans would harm. We live and we learn through awen (Welsh word, meaning flowing or poetic inspiration, more on that later), through inspiration from nature.

You can be a Druid whether or not you belong to an Order, a Grove, or any other formalised group. Following the path of Druidry means honouring the natural world and all within it, developing a relationship and seeking to work with the world in harmony and in balance.

Druidry is all about working in the world, being in the here and now. It is very much a pathway that is based upon what you do, not what you say or what title and credentials you claim. It is experiential and physical. It broadens the mind and intellect, and it will not allow you to rest on your laurels.

Druidry takes the environment into consideration on so many levels. Many Druids are animistic, believing in the essential and inherent spirit of everything, whether it be rock or tree, raindrop, beetle, horse or the sea. There is a sense of consciousness in everything. When I use the word consciousness, I don't mean in the scientific sense of the last two centuries, where it was used to differentiate between humans and animals as well as "non-sentient" beings. Consciousness in this regard is a part of the greater web of life, where threads are woven together, separate but still connected. It is what makes something what it is – whether it is a rose, a cloud or the moon. It is its own inherent identity or, more poetically, its own song that makes it different. It is spirit given form.

With that sense of consciousness in all things, it is much harder for the Druid to disregard any aspect of the environment. No longer are wildflowers plucked for their beauty, to die within days on our dining room table. No longer is it an option to squash the spider in the living room seeking warmth from the coming winter. Our entire perception is changed once we view the environment and each individual thing as having its own consciousness. We gain both a greater and broader view of the web of existence, at the same time as finding our own place within it.

This world view brings with it a responsibility. No longer are we allowed to remain ignorant of the ways of our own environment. If we are to view it as a whole, then we must truly see every part that we also play within it. If the whole of nature has a spirit, then issues arise such as the taking of a life for food. Many within Druidry are vegetarian, if not vegan, and yet there are still others who eat the flesh of animals. Some do so claiming that ethically raised and slaughtered animals for food are perfectly acceptable to put on our plates. It is entirely your choice. We must accept responsibility for whatever part we choose to play. We must research and sacrifice our ignorance of a subject before coming to a conclusion while living in service to the land.

The word environment, however, has many meanings. Our immediate response to the word is the natural environment – nature. Yet there are many other environments – little worlds created by human consciousness. We have our work environment, our home environment, our communities, villages, towns and cities. There is the issue of human-to-human inter-action as well as interaction with nature (though as humans are a part of nature, I realise that I am contradicting myself in some ways, but please bear with me). Our own sense of self, or self-awareness, creates a thorny path down which we must navigate carefully in order not to injure ourselves or others. Unless one lives as a hermit, the Druid will have interaction with other human beings, some Druids, some not. Taking, for example, the Druid relationship with nature, sensing the inherent consciousness within it, Druidry teaches us that same sense of consciousness exists in human-to-human interactions.

Within Druidry, there is a beautiful Welsh word: awen. Various meanings range from flowing water to divine or poetic inspiration. I prefer the inspirational route; however, this is not an out-of-the-blue inspirational experience, but one that is crafted through time and dedication to one's environment. We develop a rapport with both nature and inspiration itself, until they both work hand in hand. To the Druid, inspiration lies all around us in the environment, whatever environment that may be.

The word "inspiration" means to breathe in. Breathing in must, of course, be followed by breathing out – exhalation. Breathing is the most primitive and simplest way we relate to our environment, and the most effective way of remembering that we are a part of it. The air that we breathe is also the air our ancestors breathed 50, 100, 1,000 years ago. It is also the air that the willow, alder and yew trees exhaled 50, 100 or 1,000 years ago. The wasp breathes in the same air, the grasses and wildflowers exhaling into the deepening twilight. We can relate to our environment by simply remembering how to breathe, what we breathe and how it is all connected. From that, we literally gain inspiration, as well as being inspired by it. The inspired Druid then exhales that inspiration, whether it be a song to the darkening skies before a thunderstorm, giving thanks before partaking in a meal, writing a symphony, throwing paint at a wall, organising a protest against fracking or dancing in the light of the moon. This establishes a communication between the Druid and the environment – speaking to each other, even if it is without words.

We relate to our environment though inspiration, and we are all related to each other. It isn't simply communication with our environment, but a soul-deep sense of relativity – we are all related. By being related, this instils within us a sense of responsibility, of caring for the environment. If we see that we are related to the badgers living in the brownfield area soon to be redeveloped, then we also see that we must take action to ensure that they are safe. If we see that we are related to the food that we eat, we will ensure that we eat organically and, if possible, grow our own food as much as we can to develop that relationship even further. If we see that we are related to our neighbour next door, we are more likely to establish an honourable connection to them and the rest of the community. It creates a sense of caring for the environment and all within it.

The challenge that faces the Druid is to see clearly these relationships, and to act honourably in all regards. If this challenge is accepted, then our worldview is broadened considerably. The web of life will shimmer with inspiration along every thread. The solitary Druid walks this path alone, with the birds and the trees as their guides, with the ancestors and deities and the natural world forming a part of their worldview and teaching. It is the personal responsibility of the solitary Druid to learn all that she or he can, whether it is from history books or thunderstorms, music-making or love-making. All that we experience in life can be our teachers, if we choose to listen. It is about waking up the world again and again, so that we never take it, or anything, for granted inasmuch as is humanly possible. The solitary Druid is responsible for this personal awakening, time and time again. In developing a relationship with the world, we can immerse ourselves deeper within it, acknowledging the sanctity of all things.

Chapter Three

Druidry and the Awen

In Druidry, we often hear the word "awen" being used, but what exactly is awen? We've heard it briefly mentioned in the previous chapter, but now we will take a closer look at it.

Loosely translated from Welsh, it means flowing or poetic spirit, or flowing/poetic inspiration. Awake to our own energy, and stretching out towards the energy of nature around us, we begin to see just what awen is. It is an opening of one's self, of one's spirit or soul, in order to truly and very deeply see into the nature of all beings and, indeed, to see into the nature of simply being. When we are open, we can receive that divine gift, the inspiration that flows whether it is from deity, nature, or whatever it is that you choose to focus on.

For awen to exist, there must be relationship. We cannot be inspired unless we are open, and we cannot be open unless we have established a relationship, whether that is with the thunder, the blackbird or a god. Awen is cyclical in nature; we open and give of ourselves and in doing so we receive in a continuous cycle. Letting go, releasing ourselves into the flow of awen allows it to flow ever more freely. We find ourselves inspired not only in fits and bursts of enlightenment or inspiration, but at all times, carrying that essence of connection and wonder with us in our everyday lives.

But just what is awen? It is an awareness, not just on a physical and mental level, but also on a soul-deep level of the entirety of existence, of life itself. It is seeing the threads that connect us all. It is the deep well of inspiration that we drink from, to nurture our souls and our world and to give back in joy, in reverence, in wild abandon and in solemn ceremony.

Many group and solitary Druid rituals may begin or end with

singing or chanting the awen. When doing so, the word is stretched to three syllables, sounding like ah-oo-wen. It is a lovely sound that opens up the heart and soul. (Personally, I prefer to chant or sing it as it sounds when spoken – to each their own on the solitary path!) Sung/chanted it simply flows, as its namesake determines. Our hearts literally can open if we let them when we chant or sing the awen.

Yet the awen may be different for each and every Druid. The connection, and the resulting expression of that connection (the Druid's own creativity), can be so vast and diverse. It is what is so delicious about it – we inhale the awen and exhale our own creativity in song, in dance, in books, in protest marches – the possibilities are endless, as is the awen itself. For the solitary Druid, the awen knows no bounds.

Within Druidry, we learn to work with awen, with inspiration and the flow of life itself, to see where we fit in the grand scheme of things. We work to see how we can live with the least harm to ourselves and the planet, and also what we can do to make the world a better place. We work to create peace within ourselves and peace in the outer world as well. Using our natural abilities and skills, we may work with songs and poetry, or with visions or herbal medicine, with roles in teaching and counselling, in law or in environmentalism – the list is endless. We are devoted to helping and conserving nature and our planet, sharing the awen and giving back for what we have received. Awen implies service.

When out walking in the forest, we can lose our sense of self in order to become the forest. Once we are the forest, we are able to drink deeply from the flow of awen that is all life around us. We become the trees, the deer, the fox, the boulder, the streams and the badger. We can learn so much from this integration. When we are fully immersed in simply "being", we are fully in the flow of awen.

Our footsteps become lighter, our passage barely noticeable.

Like the deer, we are able to bound through the trees, awake and aware to every sense. Indeed, all our senses become sharper, clearer, for our minds are not running us ragged thinking about what to have for dinner, the paper that is due or the meeting we have on Monday. Fully in the moment, we become the awen.

Awen is also compassion. Compassion is trying to understand, to see the bigger picture, to be inspired to be a part of an integrated and integral life; living gently, gracefully and with kindness. Many people misinterpret compassion, seeing it as weakness, or perhaps being a bit of a pushover. Why be kind to others when so few are kind to us? Living with compassion is what enables us to connect once again to that all-important word in Druidry – awen. The songs of life can only be heard if we try to understand them. We cannot understand them unless we open ourselves in compassion, to truly hear them with an open heart.

In one of the Grail legends, Perceval reaches the wounded Fisher King and is invited into his castle. The knight does not ask the King why he is wounded, or how it happened. He shows no interest in learning the story behind the wounded King, no compassion. Upon sharing a meal with the King, the knight also sees a courtly procession whereby a young maiden carries the Grail through the hall repeatedly throughout the night. Again, trying to appear worldly and nonchalant, Perceval does not query this occurrence. These two incidents are the clues whereby the Fisher King might be healed, and in which Perceval failed at his chance in finding the Grail. If he had only asked the King, "What ails thee?" then the King would have been instantly and magically healed. If Perceval had only asked, "Whom does the Grail serve?" he would have understood its purpose, and achieved the totality of his quest.

The simple question, "What ails thee?" is the showing of compassion. It is taking ourselves outside of our own minds and our own troubles and asking another person what is wrong, seeking to alleviate their suffering. Also, by asking our selves (the separation of the words, instead of writing "ourselves" is intentional here), "What ails thee?" we take the time to look within, to perhaps explore shadow aspects of being. Within many Eastern traditions, it is through meditation that we understand our selves better, and also understand and redirect our reactions to the world – i.e. instead of simply reacting to an event, we act with intention, with mindfulness and awareness. With the Grail question, we can ask this of our selves as well as others in pretty much any situation, thereby eliminating a reactionary response for a more intentional approach. In doing so, we may just find the healing for our selves and the world that is so needed.

The second Grail question, "Whom does the Grail serve?" invites us to question our intention. Whether we are experiencing pleasant or unpleasant aspects in our lives, we can ask our selves, "Who does this serve?" thereby eliminating that which is no longer necessary, and bringing joy, awe and wonder back into our lives. With old habits and patterns of behaviour that we wish to be freed from, we can simply ask this question over and over again until we have the answer that is required for spiritual growth. We can ask this question in every aspect of our lives, from our weekly shopping (in order to make better choices not only for ourselves, but also the planet) to our everyday interactions with other people. If we are making a positive change instead of falling into negative but comfortable patterns then we are on the road to spiritual progress. Reminding our selves of the Grail questions can become a mantra for everyday life, filling our lives with awen.

In our quest for wholeness, for awen, we can either run around in circles, questing after the Grail through established means, or we can simply look within to gain a better perspective on compassion and the divine, whether it be male or female, or even genderless. It is the deep exploration within that allows us to bring that knowledge out into the world – we cannot simply spend our lives gazing at our own navels; we must bring the

Grail out for the benefit of others. We must offer the gifts of compassion, self-awareness and awen.

We can learn the values of compassion, and we can also look deep within for the inspiration to live an integrated life that reflects the natural cycles of the world around us. When we do that, we do not simply touch the awen every now and then – we become the awen ourselves.

Chapter Four

The Gods in Druidry

In Druidry, there is a broad interpretation of just who or what the gods are. Some Druids are monotheists, believing in only one god. Some are polytheists, believing in many gods. Some are pantheists, believing that everything is an interpretation of the divine, and this seems to bridge the two strands of monotheism and polytheism. A benefit of the solitary path is that we can choose our own path, which may or may not lead to relationship with deity or deities. We may choose to see Druidry as a religion, with deity concepts, or see it as a philosophy, and leave deity out of it. We can choose to work with certain gods, or pantheons, if we so wish. As solitaries, we are not restricted to certain deities or pantheons. But who are the gods in Druidry?

Most often we begin with gods from Celtic pantheons, as our pre-Christian precursors in Britain and parts of Europe would have known. There are Irish, Welsh, Brythonic and Gallic deities that could all fall under the heading of "Celtic". The term Celtic is constantly undergoing revision, as history turns up new theories and evidence as to just who the Celts were. Then again, there are other pre-Christian traditions often revered in Druidry, such as those of the Norse and Anglo-Saxons, and other religions from around the world. Druidry is not confined to the British Isles or Europe.

There is no single authority telling us who our god is, or what She is saying, in solitary Druidry, or indeed in Druidry as a whole. There are books, teachers, Orders, Groves etc. that can offer paths of a tradition that may lead to a relationship with the gods, but again they won't tell you exactly who they are – we're given a map and a compass, but we have to find our own way.

There are so many classifications of deity in Druidry.

25

Ancestral gods, those who have been revered by a particular tribe or people for a substantial length of time, may still dwell alongside those who have formed a relationship with them in their original environment. Ancestral gods may also travel thousands of miles when people relocate to other parts of the world, bringing their culture and identity with them. These ancestral gods may be heroes out of legend and myth, elevated to godhood. They may be physical manifestations of natural phenomena. They may be real, or they may be archetypes.

Other gods can be found in the place wherein one lives. Where I live near the coast, the gods sing their songs in the wind and rain – sometimes warm and refreshing from the south, or bitter and cold from the north. There are the gods of forest and heath, and also of farming and agriculture. There are ancestral gods of place, the local environment as well, that we can see reflected in old place names. Town and village names may often reflect a deity that was worshipped in that specific location. Finding out about local deities is not only great fun, but an essential part of Druidry and working with the land upon which we live. For the solitary Druid, this learning forms the basis for their Druidry, as having a relationship with the land is such a large part of their spiritual path.

Then there are the gods of humanity – those of love and lust, of rage and anger, of compassion and fidelity. They sing deep within our bones, and are just as much a force to be reckoned with as the other gods. The Druid works to establish relationship with these gods as much as with the gods of nature – for humans are a part of nature. We need to understand ourselves in order to understand the world, and find our place in it.

Often the gods of wilderness are honoured within Druidry. The word conjures up images of windswept moors and heathland, dark tangling forests and craggy mountaintops. It is the spirit of the untamed, the uncivilised; the spark that humanity cannot touch, much in the same way as deity is traditionally viewed. For many Druids, that wilderness is deity – it has the power to give and sustain life or the power to kill. It has not and, in many places, cannot be touched by human hands, existing without any human interference. That same dark spark exists within our own human souls as well, offering us the sanctity of the wilderness within.

As wilderness flows with the cycles, it shows that it cares little about anything else. It exists to exist – there is no other. It follows its own song, and will continue to do so. Humans may interfere with the existing wilderness, "taming" it if you will, but it will continue to carry on attempting to restore itself to its original state. It is that spirit, that sense of soul song reclaiming itself again and again that is so fascinating. The weeds will continue to sprout in the garden; the wind will continue to blow regardless of skyscrapers, bridges, mountaintops or 500-year-old yew trees.

This could be seen as thoughtless – and, when examining it closer, it is. Nature does not think – it simply does. The rose blooms because that is what it does, the fox destroys the hen house because that is what it does. When we humans enter (albeit very briefly) a state of grace where we dissolve and simply do (giving birth, or meditating, for example), we experience this whole other realm of existence. When we enter this state, we come very much closer to our gods. This can also be attained through a deep understanding and relationship to awen.

How we treat the wilderness both within and without should be made with respect to the gods of the wild places. If wilderness is viewed as deity, then our whole perception of it is changed. We may leave it alone – as deity can kill. We may work to protect it, fighting fiercely for it like one of our own. However, any way we look at it, we look at it with new respect. We honour its song.

My personal treatment of these wild places is to leave no trace of my human passing, should I venture into an area of

wilderness. Taking a pedantic view, no area will ever be the same
– our footprints tread on beetles under leaves, our passage
destroying the spider's web spanning from branch to branch.
However, nothing is ever the same – life is continually
happening: being born, being created, living and dying all
around us. My aim in life is to honour this cycle, most apparent
in the wilderness of the landscapes around me, as well as the
wilderness in my own soul. You don't mess with the gods. You
don't sublimate to them either. We may seek to understand, to
establish communication, a relationship with them, but we
should not interfere in their song in these places where it is so
strong, so precious. For it is in these places where we see clearly
the divinity within nature, and in doing so see the nature of the
divine.

There is a certain anthropocentricity to the human mind. We
often believe, or act as though, we are at the centre of the
universe. Why should we be the recipients of all that we perceive
to be good in the world, and why do we rail against the perceived
tragedy? Yes, an earthquake is devastating, and can kill
thousands of people, causing pain and anguish among humanity,
and all other creatures that suffer from its effects. But the earthquake is not at fault (pardon the pun) – that is the nature of the
earthquake. It will not seek out a place where it can cause the
least destruction, nor vice versa – it happens where it needs to
happen, where the elements dictate it should be, where the song
takes it. It does not consider the repercussions it will have on
anything. Nature is not beneficent just for us. The Wild Gods are
not there for our benefit.

We often anthropomorphise the deities of nature in order to be
able to relate to them better. It can be easier to talk to a god of
thunder, who struts around wielding a great hammer against
giants, than it is to talk to a thundercloud, or the lightning. These
gods, who we have given human form – do they care for us?

By giving them some sort of humanity, we automatically

assume that they should. After all, they look like us, talk like us, have adventures that we can relate to. We have shared these wonderful stories about them. We care for them, we devote ourselves to them – should they not do the same? Well, some do, some do not.

This can often be the falling down point in relationships with the gods for many people. I have known people who have abandoned the gods because they have lost loved ones, or had other trauma in their lives that the gods did not intercede in. My question would be – why should they intercede? There can be the assumption that the gods are "on call" for us, for our whims and demands and pleas for help.

They are not.

I have relationships with several gods, to help me understand them and the ways of the world a little better, but I know that I am not special. What I hope to achieve through my relationship with the gods is a better understanding of the bigger picture in life, beyond my own mortal limitations, in order to better my own situation and that of the world at large. As a Druid I work to find balance, harmony and truth in all that I do.

A goddess like Brighde I care very deeply for, and I see the reflection of that love and care in Her own being, poured out to the world. She cares for many, many people as many care for Her. It is in that relationship where we are reflected in each other that brings us closer to our gods, and vice versa – not because we have achieved some special status or said a set number of prayers and daily devotions. Unlike the Wild Gods, these gods appear to be more concerned with humanity as well as the world. It can often be easier to relate to these gods simply for that reason.

Many gods interact with humans on a regular basis, in a loving and caring way. Within the Celtic pantheon, there is the great mother goddess of all, Danu, who is deeply revered and honoured for all that she bestows on the gods and humans alike.

Dagda, sometimes called The Good God, is loved by many for his relationship to humanity. Gods from other pantheons, like Thor, are the champions of humanity against the wild forces (sometimes of nature) that are pitted against them.

However we choose to see the gods, the method in which we honour them is entirely up to us. We have the choice on the solitary path to really work deeply with the deities that call to us personally, to see where the most honourable relationship lies, freed from any restrictions that could be imposed by working with a group. A single word of caution, however – it is best to stick to a set pantheon, as gods from differing pantheons might not work well together.

For other Druids, there is no need for deity within their path. They simply see no need to deify the forces of nature in order to relate to them. There are atheist Druids and agnostic Druids. In the true spirit of Druidry, however, one would never, ever, mock another's belief, or lack of belief in deity, nor hold it in contempt or condemnation. To do so is anathema within Druidry – we all walk our own paths.

Chapter Five

The Ancestors in Druidry

We can often think of a solitary path as a lonely one. When we have gained a greater understanding of the world we live in, we see that we can never truly be alone. For the Druid, there are so many levels of interconnectedness that we can tap into for inspiration along the path's journey. Connecting with the ancestors is just one way – there are many others.

When people think of the ancestors, the first thing that comes to mind is blood relatives from the past. In Druidry, we honour not only our blood ancestors, but also those ancestors of tradition (those who have shared our worldviews) and of place (those who are a part of our land). Yet it is not only the ancestors of the past that concern us – it is ancestors of the future, those yet to come, who we must consider and which I will touch upon briefly here before exploring the subject later on in this book.

I am childless by choice. I will not have direct descendants, though I share my genetic makeup with the rest of my family, my nephews, cousins and more, which will be passed down through blood. However, I will become a future ancestor of tradition as well as having future ancestors of tradition, and the same can be said for being and having future ancestors of place. It is mostly to these ancestors yet to come, my future ancestors of all three groups, that direct the way in which I live my life.

Our ancestors of the past have helped to shape us, to make us what we are, though we are our own person and always have our own choices to make in life. We can repeat past mistakes or we can change – it is up to us. Our ancestors of the future do not have the luxury of choice – they are stuck with whatever it is that we provide them. With the world being in such a mess, alongside the moments of pure beauty I worry about what I will leave for them.

Emma Restall Orr, a prolific Druid author, states on her website that she endeavours to live a life of which her ancestors would be proud. That is a beautiful and motivating sentiment – and is especially poignant for our future ancestors. We have the option of learning from our previous ancestors to make this world a better place, in however big or small a way, for our future ancestors. Apathy has no place in the Druid worldview – everything we do matters.

I have made mistakes in my past. I have had glorious achievements. I can acknowledge all of these, and today be the best person I can be, for the sake of my future ancestors of blood, tradition and place. There is no time to wallow in guilt, or to rest on my laurels – every single deed, every single action right now will have an effect on the future. The past is there to teach us, the future is there to direct us, and the present moment exists to capture all that we can be in this moment in time.

Our ancestors of blood are those who normally come to mind first. We think of our family trees, spanning back hundreds of years. Yet our ancestors of blood are also those who are still alive, and those of our blood who have yet to come. Our mothers and fathers, sisters and brothers, cousins, aunts and uncles are all ancestors of blood. Also, our children, our nieces, nephews, second cousins and so on are our ancestors of blood – some may not have even been born yet, but they all share in our blood line. Honouring the ancestors is restrictive if we simply have a linear view of time – expand that a bit further and a whole new world of blood ancestors opens up, from our ancestors dating back hundreds of thousands of years, and even before we were classified as human.

In honouring the ancestors of blood, we see that in essence we are all related. With the gift of consciousness, the homo sapiens sapiens (the beings that are aware that they are aware) are able to see the world in a different light, should they choose to do so. Being conscious that we are all related can lead to a sense of peace, as well as an end to war, racism, sexism and so on.

Our blood ancestors from the past have made us who we are, at least physically. They may have bestowed upon us other gifts as well – artistic ability, exceptional maths ability, or an ability to sing in perfect tone and pitch. What we are right now will be carried to our ancestors of the future, whether or not we even have our own children. Our blood is mixed with that of everyone else on the planet. In a sense, there is no "last of the line" when viewed in this manner. There is no fear that we need to procreate to continue the line in our already over-populated world.

Honouring our blood ancestors can also bring about peace. It can connect us to our most recent relatives, and also heal the wounds created by any discord, strife or grief that have occurred. Where violence or abuse have taken place, coming to terms with the blood line can bring about great healing. It can be the most difficult thing one has ever done. You may not have to even like the person, but you can see the shared blood and make the change in behaviour if you need to do so. Acknowledging what has happened can have tremendous power. Even if forgiveness is not possible, acknowledgement always is.

Ancestors of place are those who have shared the same physical space that we currently reside in. It could mean our homes, our communities, our country, our continent. Some of the wilder places may not have many human ancestors of place, but do we need to limit ourselves to just those of the human race? If we live in the wilds of northern Canada, where few humans have ever lived, we can honour those few humans who have, and also those spirits who have made their home there for ages – the bear, the wolf, the squirrel, the caribou. Looking at ancestors of place in this light can be fascinating.

Some places have older human connections, such as here in the UK. In honouring the spirits of place, we can not only acknowledge those who built our house, or our village or town, but also those who first settled in these lands. With wave after wave of people coming into the British Isles, there are many to choose from: Saxon, Roman, Norman, Norse, Celt and so on. With a very strong and long line of human history, the possibilities are almost endless in a country rich with human heritage.

Knowing that one day we will also be ancestors of place gives us a responsibility to maintain our human habitats to the best of our abilities. It means looking out not only for ourselves and our community but also the entire planet. Our future ancestors are, after all, the ones who will inherit. Being spirits of place we can have an effect on the present and the future by having organic gardens, recycling or even keeping bees. Investigating the land upon which you live is a wonderful exercise in honouring these ancestors. Find out who lived there before you and how they lived. Find out what you can do to honour them, and how you can leave a great legacy that will improve your own place, whether that is your own little plot or the whole planet itself.

Often, the ancestors of tradition can become relegated to the back-burner; most often when people think of ancestors it is those of their family lines that they think of. Also, ancestors of place can take precedence in a setting where their songs are still widely sung and heard in the deepening twilight. The ancestors of tradition, however, will always hold a special place in our hearts if we make room for them.

Some people may have inspired us on our spiritual and religious path. They may not even have been of the same spirituality or religion, but share ideals held in common. Oftentimes, these can be seen as the more prominent people of the traditions, those who have garnered a supposed "higher" status due to their position, their accomplishments and their deeds. The cult of celebrity is rampant even among us pagans. Some are widely known not only for their virtue, but because of who they are – the Dalai Lama for example. Others have been known by the virtue of their deeds (not to say the Dalai Lama isn't worthy) and examples that spring to mind are Mother Theresa or Dr Martin

Luther King Jr. All these people can be ancestors of tradition if we hold the same beliefs, morals and attitudes as they do, even though they are not necessarily pagan or Druidic.

Celebrity pagans abound now due to social media, the increase of pagan books being published and television/radio appearances. These people who the media seeks out for whatever reason can be seen as ancestors of tradition. We may not like what they are saying or representing, but they have become the spokespeople others are listening to. This can be disheartening when you don't agree with their principles or the execution of shared principles. It can also result in elation when there is agreement – "Yes, someone *important* is saying what I've been saying all along, what needs to be said, what needs to be done," etc. Whether we choose to honour them or not is our decision.

Just because someone has written a book, or ten books, or appeared on television, newspapers or the radio, doesn't make them any more noteworthy than the pagan who quietly picks up litter by the roadside and sings to the sunset in her organic garden. It is the cult of celebrity that has changed our perceptions. We may take inspiration from acclaimed authors whose words strike a chord in our hearts – equally, we may take inspiration from the pagan family in the next town over that hosts seasonal celebrations in their backyard for all in the community.

Honour should not be bestowed simply because of celebrity. Equally, honour should be bestowed from within as well as from without. In honouring your very own self as part of a spiritual or religious tradition, you also honour those in whose footsteps you may follow, whose words we listen for on the dawn's solar wind.

When we acknowledge the ancestors within Druidry, we are never alone.

Chapter Six

The Eight Festivals of the Year

In Druidry, we celebrate eight festivals that fall roughly equidistant to each other in the calendar year. We may follow the dates set in the calendar, or we may choose to work with the markers of the seasons, as nature tells us when and where to celebrate each festival. Living in the United Kingdom, these often fall fairly close to each other, as it was a system created in Britain for a developing paganism (for more on how the eight festivals were created, see Ronald Hutton's books listed in the bibliography). As a solitary Druid, it is entirely your choice as to when and how you wish to celebrate these festivals. Below are a few guidelines that are generally accepted by Druids throughout Britain – for Druids living in the southern hemisphere, the seasonal celebrations can be flipped to accord with what is happening in nature on the other side of the equator.

We begin in the dark of winter, at the Winter Solstice, which occurs between the 20th and 22rd of December. This is the longest night of the year, and the tide is about to turn to lengthening days with more sunlight. In Britain, where the days can be terribly short, especially on dark, overcast wintry days, this shift towards the light half of the year is very remarkable and special for some people – not least those who suffer from Seasonal Affective Disorder. It is a time of darkness, of quiet contemplation and of family. Bringing sprigs of greenery into the home to decorate the hearth and integrate the natural world with the inner sanctums, and the giving of gifts that is now traditional at this time of year, strengthens the family and community bonds. It is a time for rest, as the earth lies dormant, seeds waiting below the ground for the return of the sun as the cold winds blow.

At Imbolc we welcome the lengthening days and the first of

the flowers, with the snowdrops coming into season. For those who celebrate by the calendar, Imbolc occurs on the 2nd of February. Some prefer to celebrate when the snowdrops are out, finding this more in tune with the season. This could happen anytime from beginning of January to mid February, depending on the winter. Imbolc is also the time when the sheep begin to produce milk – ewe's milk – which is where we get the name Imbolc from. For our ancestors this was a celebratory time, when cheese and butter could once again be made to replenish the winter stores. Again, the milking time can occur any time from the start of February onwards – whenever it happens, it is always a joy to watch the fields and wait to see the new lambs scampering and flipping their tails. This is a time for preparing the seeds of what we wish to achieve in the coming year, dreamt up over the long winter nights, but not yet ready to plant – we must still keep these dreams safe.

The Spring Equinox (21 - 22 March) is one of two very special times of balance and of change. It is a liminal time, a time that hovers between two realities, waiting to see what will befall. The balance is changing, and just after this liminal time the day prevails over the night. The days become longer than the nights, the sun rising and setting ever further apart along the horizon. It is a time of change – we can stand on the precipice, waiting to see what happens, until we lose our balance, are pushed or jump headlong into our lives. The greening is just about to happen – nature is about to explode in riotous growth with blossoms beginning to appear. It was also the hungry time of year for our ancestors – when the winter stores were running very thin, and the crops in the fields were not yet ready. Food was scarce, and spring claimed more deaths than winter ever could for those who lived off the land. The year lies before us with the promise of spring and at this changeable time, we determine the course of the light half of the year inasmuch as we can in our own lives, and sow the seeds that will bring about change.

At Beltane, or May Day on the 1st of May, all life rejoices in fertility. The hawthorn, or May bush, is usually in bloom at this time of year, and in nature we see the beautiful mating game, the dance and the courtship that will hopefully produce something wonderful later in the year. The sap is rising in the trees and in our own blood, and we feel rejuvenated, alive in the beauteous glory that the coming summer will bring. It is a time of expression – a reminder of the cycle, in that every inhale must have an exhale, and so we release ourselves into the tides of summer, riding the waves of energy that pulsate through the land. At this time of year we are all young, no matter what our years. It is a celebration of fertility in nature and in our very souls, where the awen flows clear, light and strong.

At Midsummer, or the Summer Solstice (20 - 22 June), we revel in the time of longest light – the days seem to linger forever, the twilight hours bringing cool release from the heat of the day, and the very short nights giving way to early dawns. The sun is at its peak, and so too can we feel the same way at this time of year. Honouring the cycle of the sun is important in Druidry, and we reflect the times and tides of nature in our own lives so that we can better attune ourselves to the world around. This is also a challenging time, for those sensitive to the light, or heat – it is a time for the making or breaking of a soul, much like the Winter Solstice. The tides are constantly changing, and though we may be at our height, our fall is yet to come.

At the beginning of August (1 August if celebrating by the calendar) is Lughnasad, or Lammas, the celebration of the cutting of the first crop. It is a time to see the product of our labours since the long dreaming and introspection of winter. If we have worked hard, and external factors beyond our control have been beneficial, then what we have sown in the spring should now start to come to fruition. The flowers are out in full force, the trees swaying in the breeze, and the long dog days of August lie ahead. There is no time to stop, as we must still keep at our labour for our harvest to be fruitful. It is a time for exchange and trade as well – for at this time the Celtic ancestors gathered to celebrate the first harvest with festivals honouring not only the time of year, but also to honour community and family. Love that bloomed in the spring came to marriage in August, vows were exchanged, goods and labour agreed upon.

The Autumn Equinox (20-22 September) brings us again to that point of balance where we wait upon the knife's edge for the tide to turn to the dark half of the year, when the nights become longer than the days. The leaves are beginning to change, the nights are chill and the best of the flowers have gone. Nature is slowly winding down, and animals are beginning their migrations. The tractors and combine harvesters are out in full force, gathering the crops of onions, turnips and cereals. The fallow deer are beginning to come together in larger herds for the winter – all are making preparations for the colder months. Our ancestors did as much as they could to prepare for the winter, and so too should we – even in our much easier, gentler existence. Our ancestors needed to come together at this time of year to ensure they made it through the dark days of winter. So too must we come together to see that the impact we make upon this planet, our home, is for the benefit of all, and not just the few, or our own selves. We must share in the bounty that we have harvested.

Samhain, Hallowe'en, All Soul's Night (31 October) – for many pagans this is the ending of one year and the beginning of another. It is often seen as the third and final harvest – with the last of the apples harvested, the cattle were prepared for winter and the grain stored properly. It is also a time when it is said that the veil between the worlds is thin, and the realms of the living and the dead are laid bare to each other. We are approaching the darkest time of the year, and the killing frosts and snows await just around the corner. It is a time of letting go, of releasing into the dark half of the year, and getting rid of the dross in our lives so that we do not have to carry it with us through the long winter nights. We consciously make the effort to live better, meaningful lives and let go of all that holds us back – our fears and worries, our anger and hatred. We nurture the beneficial and the good that we have in our lives, ensuring that they are well kept for our plans to come at the Winter Solstice. So the cycle continues.

Celebration and acknowledgement of these eight festivals makes up a large part of the solitary Druid's path. It is a reflection of the natural cycle of the year, and is our greatest teacher. We become inspired by what we see happening within nature, and work to keep that relationship strong and steady throughout the year, in order to bring honesty and integrity into our practice. In doing so, we walk the path in harmony with the natural world.

Section Two

Druidry in Practice

The solitary Druid seeks a connection with the natural world at his or her own pace, and on his or her own terms. There are many ways of establishing this connection, such as through meditation, prayer and sustaining our relationship to the natural world through following the seasonal cycle of the year in our own lives. This section of the book will show you how to connect to the world around you, and how to walk the Druid path in your own way.

Chapter Seven

Meditation

The very first thing we must learn to do is to keep our feet firmly on the ground. Meditation helps us with this. There are several types of meditation, which I will describe here. Like the stone settling into the depths of the pond after being thrown, so too do our bodies and souls settle after meditation. From there, we can get a clearer grasp of our place in the world.

Meditating alone is brilliant in that we have much less distraction than in group meditation. I have participated in group meditation where people have often fallen asleep – even snoring! It is hard to focus during these moments, especially if you have just begun on your meditative path. The blessing of the solitary path is just that – you move forward at your own pace with minimal distraction.

With any meditation, it helps to begin with a focus. When beginning on the path of meditation, breathing is usually the first thing we relearn how to do. We learn to become aware of our breath once again, really feeling our lungs expanding and contracting, the coolness of the air, the moisture or the dryness of it. We feel it going through our noses (I prefer to breathe through my nose in meditation – for me it is quieter and I think it is better to use our natural filters in our noses), we feel it tingling past our nostril hairs, down into our throat and lungs, feeling the expansion of our chest, the contraction of our upper backs, our diaphragm pushed down. Equally, we acknowledge the exhalation – the warm air travelling from our lungs and throat out of our noses, our diaphragms moving upwards again, the expansion of the upper back. We may even count our breaths, in sets of three, or nine, or ten – yet again I simply prefer to focus on the breath, for I believe that counting is still engaging our brains into repetitive patterns that we are trying to avoid – we are still hearing that voice in our head counting, which makes it more difficult to hear anything else.

The first few breaths we take in meditation are glorious – we are fully aware of the process, feeling it through our bodies, really engaging with what was once an automatic response to our need for air. But the novelty wears off so very quickly, with our minds so accustomed to distraction. Living with television and the internet, radio and other media, we are constantly absorbing information, doing multiple things at once, dropping one thing and heading over to the next stimulus. In meditation, we learn to be without the man-made stimulus that we have grown so accustomed to.

And so, our minds instantly wander, reliving what happened in the office today, what our lover said to us this morning, what we are going to have for dinner. Appointments, engagements, things to do – all these suddenly surface and before you know it, we've lost our focus on our breath. So we return our focus as soon as we realise we have lost it. This happens, again and again. It may happen ten times in one session, it may happen one hundred times, but it will happen.

This is where discipline kicks in. We are not trying to empty our minds. For now, we are simply trying to find a focus that will lead towards a path of stillness. We are wanting to open the door to awareness, but first we must focus our intent, grab hold of the doorknob and turn it before we can enter into the next phase. We focus on our breathing, allowing that to inspire us, literally and figuratively.

Mindfulness or Sitting Meditation

Sitting in meditation with awareness transcends into every aspect of your life. It's so hard, and yet so simple – sitting for at least 15 minutes to half an hour each day, in total awareness. At first it's really hard not to fidget – trying to get comfortable, the mind is doing everything it can to move the body so that we don't have to feel this very moment, in all its glory or mundaneness. That is the biggest hurdle – the sitting still part. At this point we can use the techniques we have gained from following our breath to help us settle down. Eventually, we want to leave the breath and just focus on sitting still. Sometimes I simply can't, and then return to a focus on the breath, or if that fails, a walking meditation will take the place of sitting meditation (more on walking meditations later). However, the importance of sitting still should not be underestimated.

Sitting in stillness, we can then imagine a rock being thrown into a pond – it settles to the bottom of its own accord – and find the stillness. Then, it is time to simply "be" in the present moment. Feeling tension in the shoulders; hearing the wind howl outside, thick with rain. Hearing the tractors in the fields; the soft padding of a cat entering the room. Smelling the incense; seeing the light of the candle upon the altar. For a few brief moments it is blissful and relaxing.

Then come the thoughts – anyone who has ever tried to meditate knows the flurry of thoughts that will fly through your head at any given moment. It can sometimes be a Herculean task to just sit when all these thoughts are going through your head – if you're moving, often you don't have to think about them, or notice that they are passing through your head with lightning speed. But sitting still and facing all these thoughts – it can sometimes seem futile. I've heard so many people say, "I can't meditate – I can't turn off, switch off; I keep thinking a million things." You've got to persevere.

So, in sitting meditation, we don't try to push away all these thoughts – what we learn to do is to become the observer. It's all about noticing the thoughts that go through the mind, without attaching to them and becoming lost in them. As soon as we attach to them, we've lost our awareness, our sense of being an observer – instead we are a willing or unwilling participant in them, and we will rarely see the benefits of meditation.

The more and more you meditate, the less and less you become absorbed in your thoughts. However, there will always be good days and bad days. I have found that when I don't meditate for a few days, I can and do get lost in my thoughts, creating dramas out of them, or becoming easily annoyed with myself or other people around me – losing that sense of connectedness, compassion and empathy. This is because the benefits of sitting meditation carry through into all aspects of life – seeping through like springwater into the surrounding areas, benefiting all with its nourishment.

The more I do sitting meditation, the less irritable I am (though again, we all have good days and bad days). I am able to notice tension in my body more throughout the day, and can work with awareness to release it. I notice when I am being self-centred, or when I am losing myself in the drama that I have created to give my life more importance. Sitting meditation makes you realise that all this drama is self-created to a large extent. While some tragedies can still occur, our attachment to them will be lessened, and life flows that much easier even in the midst of major trauma or upheaval.

Walking Meditation

As a follower of Druidry on the solitary path, you have the benefit of peace and quiet found in solitude as well as being able to make your own schedule, in which to incorporate elements of Druid learning. Walking meditation is a brilliant way to honour your Druid path while at the same time honouring your very own self.

Meditation is proven to have beneficial health results and, as such, is a great tool for self-development in order to be of greater service to the world. Through meditation we come to know and understand our selves better and thereby can act accordingly in the wider world. With walking meditation, you also have the benefit of physical exercise.

When performing walking meditation, it is best to do so in an area where you don't have to think too much – for example, difficult terrain can be a hindrance to walking meditation. A simple route where you can relax and not worry about tripping up, getting lost or hit by a car is essential.

In walking meditation as in sitting meditation, the focus is brought into the self before expanding outwards. It is about truly feeling the walking, from placing one foot in front of the other, feeling the weight shift from heel to ball to toes, travelling up through the leg, the movement of the arms, following the breath. It is about feeling the pull of gravity and working against that. It is about feeling the air on your skin, the sunlight or rain upon your head and shoulders.

The aim is not to drive all other thoughts from your mind, but simply to acknowledge them when they arise. Paying attention is key. If you find your mind drifting to what happened previously during the day, return the mind to what you are doing – just walking, breathing, moving. Let the thought go without recrimination for losing your concentration and keep going.

Discipline and Benefits

Anywhere from 20 minutes to an hour is good. For those whom sitting still is either painful or just too difficult, walking meditation might be the answer. There are other forms of meditation – guided meditations, journeying, even yoga. Look into different forms of meditation to see what suits you best. Later on in this book we will incorporate guided meditation into our practice, to be performed after sitting meditation.

You have to want to meditate. People who say they cannot perhaps haven't tried hard enough, or don't want it enough in their lives. You have to be willing to commit to a certain amount of time and effort each and every day, and also to a commitment not only to change yourself, but to become more aware of yourself, and by doing so, flow through life better. You have to want to spend time alone. You have to want to get to know yourself. Obstacles will still be there, but like water we can flow around them instead of slamming into them again and again, never getting any further along the way.

Your life will become more active, and less reactive – instead of reacting to every situation, you can act with empathy and compassion. Your ability to respond well increases each and every day. It is a responsibility – the ability to respond. It is also learning discipline, to sit when you don't feel like it, to be aware when your mind and body both are rebelling against the stillness and would rather be in the made-up world of your mind instead of sitting in the reality of the here and now.

Slowly, that awareness gained through meditation will affect everything you say and do, for the better. The goal, however, is not self-improvement – the goal is to be in the here and now, this very moment in this very life, and to see the joy and wonder that it truly is. We are gifted with long lives, should nothing unforeseen happen, and minds that can be trained back into awareness – let's use them to the best of our ability. By doing so, a sense of connection to the here and now, to all the beautiful life around us, will be achieved – which makes meditation worth the effort.

Chapter Eight

Prayer

Prayer – it's a beautiful word. It looks pretty on the page; it falls softly from the lips. It's not a word to be shouted. It is a word that is deeply connected to other words, like sacred, holiness and religion. For the pagan, as in other religions and spiritualities, it is about relationship, communion; a shared experience. Going deeper, we tumble over the words and ideas associated with it – and delve into the nature of prayer.

Not all Druids pray, but a great many of them do. It is done for many reasons – a prayer for healing, a prayer of thanks, a prayer of benediction. Some do not pray – relating prayer with the Christian tradition. Prayer goes back a lot further than that. For me personally, prayer is central to my Druidry.

In a solitary path, you have many choices when it comes to prayer. You can adopt versions of prayer that sing to your own soul from other sources or you can create your own. There are no hard and fast rules when it comes to prayer, as it is so subjective.

I wake up with a prayer, as I get out of bed and stand at the window – a version of Siegfried's prayer, which has been adapted and which I discovered through the Heathen tradition. I say a prayer to honour the spirits of land, sea and sky before each meal. Before travelling, in blessing and in ritual for all manner of reasons – prayer is a part of my life. Most of the time prayers are spoken aloud, sometimes in my mind, but what matters most is a forming of thoughts and words to express myself and to hear the other side expressed as well.

For prayer is not only a one-sided thing. One cannot do all the talking, in prayer. It is like having a friend who talks and talks and never listens to you – if you are on the receiving end of that, you will get annoyed, or at the very least, disinterested very soon. Imagine being a deity, and hearing a one-sided conversation, day in and day out. I'm sure they would tune out too.

A friend of mine said, "The first prayer should always be 'thank you'." That is a beautiful sentiment. It's important to keep perspective – for remembering what we do have, especially when times are tough. It's not about being humble, though that in itself is not such a bad thing – it is about being respectful. Too often we can gobble our food without thanking the spirits of the sun and wind, of rain and soil and the multitude of beings that brought it to our table. Too often we come home, walking through the door, without thinking of the safety and comfort that our home gives us, without pausing for a moment on the threshold and saying a quiet prayer.

As an animist, prayer is a deep intention to honour the spirit of all things that share this existence with me, both the seen and unseen. The key is in the sharing. All relationships flow in more than one direction – you simply cannot have a one-sided relationship. My garden feeds me as I feed it. I tend to the needs of my community as they tend to mine. I breathe in the air that my ancestors breathed out 10, 100, 1,000 years ago. It is all connected. Prayer is honouring that connection.

The nature of prayer is to nurture a relationship. We pray to the gods of wind and rain, of love and compassion, in order that we may come to some understanding, or gain some inspiration, as well as offering thanks in return for the gifts we have already received.

So, if prayer is about connection, to the deities, the spirits of place, or whatever it is that you are praying to, then one must also stop at some point and listen. It's not a one-way conversation. We say our prayers in honour of the sunrise or sunset, or for inspiration to solve a problem, but then we must sit back and listen. Some Druids meditate after prayer, using prayer as the intention of "speaking to" and meditation as the intention of "listening to". Sometimes there is no answer – often in life, there

is no immediate answer, and we must simply find
happens. Sometimes there is no need for an answer.
taking the time to stop, to listen, even if we don't hear anything,
is to appreciate the time and place that we are sharing with
everything else on this planet. This is the other side of prayer.

So what is the nature of prayer? The nature of prayer is to
nurture, to keep strong the relationship to that which we are
praying to. It is about communion, and opening channels from
all sides in order for that relationship to happen. Another friend
said to me, which I think is beautiful is this: "Prayer is love."

Examples of Daily Prayer

Siegfried's Prayer – Adapted
Hail to the Day, and Day's Sons, Hail to Night and her Daughters
With loving eyes look upon us here and grant peace to those
    living here
Hail to the gods, Hail to the goddesses, Hail to the mighty
    fecund Earth
Eloquence and native wit bestow upon us here, and healing
    hands while we live

Serenity Prayer
God grant me the serenity to accept the things I can't change
Courage to change the things I can
And the wisdom to know the difference

Examples of Prayers of Thanksgiving

Prayer Before Meals
I give my thanks for this food that I am about to eat.
To the spirits of land, sea and sky
Know that you are honoured.

Prayer of Thanks
I give my thanks for the blessings that I have received.
I strive to walk my path with honour.
In doing so, I am reminded of the cycles of life itself.

Daily Prayer of Thanks
I give my thanks for this day
May awen and peace flow my way
In honour of this land, I pray

Example of Prayer for Help and Guidance

Prayer for Guidance
My lady (or lord, or other deity/ancestor/being) I honour you
    with all that I am.
I seek your aid – please grant me strength and inspiration in
    order to overcome this trouble.
May the awen flow through me and around me,
In the cycle of the times and tides of life.

Examples of Spontaneous Prayers

Upon Seeing the Moon
Beautiful Moon, light-bringer in the darkness
Ruler of the seas and the cycles of women
Know that you are honoured
Guide me in the darkness of night
And see my love reflected for you

In a Thunderstorm
Great gods of land, sea and sky!
Come together with energy, your songs filled with each other
Bringing rain and thunder, lightning and cloud
Restoring balance to the world
Know that you are honoured

Chapter Nine

Inner Pathworking

Inner pathworking is a tool used when we have achieved a meditative state in which we can work out problems and issues, or seek inspiration – its uses are endless. It is a form of guided meditation. We use our imagination to find our own inner world in which we are able to delve deeply into self-reflection, often challenged by those that we meet.

Once we have attained a meditative stillness, we are able to journey within the mind to meet those that may guide us, or if we have already contacted them, to a place where we can easily honour their spirit. I like to use the imagery of Glastonbury Tor, one of the holiest places in England in my personal opinion, but please feel free to adapt the inner plane/place to that which best suits you – i.e. a Canadian living in the Laurentian mountain range could adapt it to suit her locality, a Brazilian living in Rio de Janeiro would adapt it to best suit his idea of sacred space. I will use the model of Glastonbury Tor here, but please feel free to change it. If you feel the need to set up a circle of any kind before undertaking this pathworking, then feel free to do so (details of circle casting and creation of sacred space can be found in Chapter 11). Memorise or record a reading of this inner pathworking to ensure a smooth flow – pausing to read will cause disruption.

The Tor rises out of the mists of the town before you. You leave the mist-shrouded streets and come to the green tracks at the base of the Tor, looking up to the labyrinthine plateaus that spiral up towards the summit. Stopping at the two oak trees, Gog and Magog, you say a prayer and then proceed up the sacred path.

The path winds up the Tor, and you can feel that energy reflected in your own being. The sounds of nature are all around you –

skylarks or nightingales, depending upon the time of your journeying. You can feel the pulse of the earth beneath your feet as you walk, reverently placing one foot in front of the other, softly, a walking prayer upon the Goddess that is this land.

Suddenly you come across the summit – before you there is open sky. You come to the edge, just before stepping fully onto the plateau, and whisper another prayer. The prayer is taken up by the wind gods and, with a bow, you walk out onto the Tor.

The breeze plays in your hair and clothes, sometimes soft, sometimes strong. You look up at the sky, noticing the time of day, the stars or sun, moon or clouds, and what pattern they are travelling in. Taking steps forward, you reach the centre – and you see a spot where the mist is settling. Through this mist, you can see something – sometimes it is the tower of St Michael, other times the stones of an ancient stone circle appear. Sometimes the area is simply clear of all structures, sometimes nothing but mist prevails.

As you step closer to the mists, whatever you see in the centre becomes clear, as the mist lifts. A last, final sweep of mist solidifies into a figure, standing before you, waiting for your approach.

You bow reverently and walk towards the figure. The figure smiles, and introduces herself or himself to you. You introduce yourself, and then ask if this person is to be your spirit guide. If the answer is yes, then you may proceed to ask further questions, if the answer is no, then you may ask where you might find your spirit guide, and they will tell you.

Once you have asked your spirit guide your initial questions, you once again bow with reverence – they in turn bow to you. You turn to depart, and head back down the way you came, with full awareness, to your original starting point, and from there open your eyes and return to your current physical world.

Your spirit guide is there to help you on your path, so don't be shy to talk to them. Sometimes they may simply not have an answer, for there is no answer to be had. Use this inner pathworking whenever you feel the call to do so. If you are having trouble focusing in mindfulness meditation, you can always use this inner pathworking to help you find out where the agitation or trouble lies in your own soul.

The more you use inner pathworking, the more comfortable you will become with it. There are many worlds besides this physical realm, and we can access them with a little perseverance and in good faith. We must remember that doing inner pathworking is only an aid to our work in the physical realms, however, and should not be done in place of working to better our lives and the world at large through more mundane means. On the Druid path, we learn to walk between the worlds and find harmony and balance in our own lives by doing so.

Chapter Ten

Outer Pathworking

We must acquaint ourselves with the land upon which we live, as much as we come to know the inner planes. We can become too wrapped up in our own heads at times, and forget about the world around us. This exercise is designed to attune ourselves with our natural surroundings, to get us outside into the physical world of nature and develop a very real and substantial relationship with it. It can also complement our inner pathworking and make the entire process of pathworking richer and more rewarding.

At the same time every day, if possible, go out for a walk. At least 20 minutes would be ideal. Find a pace that is comfortable for you and that allows you to take in your surroundings – i.e. too fast a pace and you will not notice the little things, like a tiny bud or the first nettle peeking through the leaf mould. Feel free to stop at any point on your walk to get closer to the earth, the plants, the trees or animals if it is safe to do so. Choose two or three different routes to take, so that your walks will be slightly different, for variety's sake (as well as for personal safety, especially if you live in built-up areas).

Breathe in the air and notice the scent. Feel the wind/sun/rain on your face. Notice the temperature, the humidity. Listen to the sounds around you – human laughter, dogs barking, children shrieking, horse whinnies, tractors rolling past. You may notice or recognise other people along your walks, sharing in the pleasure of this simple act. Do not ignore them – smile, at the very least.

See what is happening seasonally around you. Are the first leaves about to burst open from the birch trees? Is the ground thick with frost? Is there the scent of woodsmoke on the wind?

What is in flower? Are there insects buzzing past?

Become familiar with the natural world of your outer pathworking. Pick up tree guides to identify the local trees, and other plant guidebooks that will help you distinguish between the various flora. Research some of the animals of the area if you are not familiar with them – i.e. if you pass some horses in a paddock each day, do a little investigation into the life of horses. Do the same if you pass a badger set, or a place where the pigeons congregate or where you find a hive of bees.

Doing this outer pathworking each and every day will connect you more fully with your landscape. You will become familiar with it, and it will come to know you. It will establish a long-lasting relationship that will ground and guide you in all your work. Remember that you are not only experiencing nature, but that nature is experiencing you. You can use the knowledge and wisdom gained to help you in your own life, as well as to work in service to the gods, the ancestors and the land.

Chapter Eleven

Altar Creation and Sacred Space

Most Druids at some point love to create an altar. The altar acts as a focal point for our workings. For those on the solitary path, this focus may be necessary in grounding and centring your practice – then again, it may not be necessary at all. The choice is entirely up to you.

If you choose to have an altar, find a suitable place, either inside, outside, or both. You may dedicate it to a particular god or goddess, or the ancestors, or the spirits of place. You may have several altars, shrines and mini temples around you. Try to perform your meditation and inner pathworking by these focal points. The familiar surroundings and atmosphere will lend themselves to your work. Fill it with photos or images, rocks, pebbles, feathers, candles, incense – whatever you heart tells you to.

Let your altar be an external part of your own self – a representation of all that you love. You will find that time spent before it is, indeed, time well spent.

The creation of sacred space is to provide us with a safe place within which to grow and transform; it is an offering of sanctuary. Sanctuary is that which gives us space where we are allowed to be ourselves, fully and without fear. It is a temple, a sacred space, both within and without. We return to the selfless source, if we so desire – a return to our true self.

There are as many different methods of casting a circle to create sacred space as there are people who are casting. Each and every method is equally valid if it works for the individual, as long as there is no harm done to oneself or others in the process. Here is how I cast a circle for ceremonial purposes (simpler circles are cast at other times) – you may come to find your own way, or already have an understanding of how you can do so yourself.

Stand facing North, holding out both arms at your sides, palms facing out. Raise both arms slowly overhead, gathering the energy of the land, sea and sky. Once both hands are overhead, bring them together to "seal" that connection with the energy, and then lower your hands in prayer position down past your face and coming to rest above your heart. Know that you are centred, with the energy of the worlds both within you and outside of you, ever-flowing. Call to your gods, if you will, to guide you, to aid you and to help hold and create this sacred space.

Next, still facing North, take your dominant hand (right hand if you are right-handed, left hand if you are left-handed) and push the energy out from your centre that you have gathered within. Next, you walk the circle's edge. Some say that you should walk clockwise, the direction of the sun, but I've always found this a little odd, as I've always moved counter-clockwise in my circles, feeling that this is the direction the Earth spins. If you look at the Earth from the North Pole, the Earth spins counter clockwise. However, the direction of the spin is relative, dependent upon where it is you are looking from on this marvellous sphere! So, to each their own...

However you walk the circle, push the energy out of your palm, creating a line waist-high of energy. I visualise this as a blue-white line of energy – you can choose the colour that best represents your own soul or need. When you have returned to the start point, close off the energy from your palm when it touches the edge of the circle from where you started. Then, as before, slowly raise your arms overhead, raising the energy and then coming into prayer position, lowering your hands before your face. When your hands are held at chest level, expand the line that you created, upwards and downwards, to turn your circle into a sphere. Sweep it around using visualisation, making it larger if necessary. You can lower the centre line of the sphere down until it touches the earth, creating a half sphere above the earth and a half sphere below the earth. Take a moment, feeling the circle/sphere that you have created. Know that this circle is an aspect of your soul.

You may then consecrate the circle with incense, to represent the elements of air, fire and earth, followed with water. Beginning at the Northern edge, walk the circle round, with a feather and censer for incense, scattering drops of water with your fingers afterwards from a bowl of water. After you have returned to where you started, the circle will have been walked three times during its creation and consecration.

Taking down the sacred circle is simply a reverse of the casting – draw the energy back into yourself and walk in the reverse direction to casting, and then when back at the North release the energy back into the land, sea and sky by reversing the hand gestures – bring your hands together at heart level and then raise them past your face, opening outwards and down to release.

If elements of this circle and sacred space casting appeal to you while others don't, then please feel free to use what works and leave out that which does not. This is your path and you should walk it accordingly, without doing anything that others tell you to that go against what you feel to be right for you. Seeking out wisdom and learning from nature and all sources is crucial, however, accepting blindly that one way is right and another is wrong can lead to all sorts of problems along your spiritual journey. May you walk your path in freedom and in respect not only for yourself but also for the world at large.

Chapter Twelve

Seasonal Rites – Working With the Seasons

Using what we have learned in the previous chapters, we can now bring them together to form our study and practice over the next cycle of the year. You can use this as a guideline for your own path, following it for a year and then see where the awen takes you...

Autumn

The harvests are coming in – now is the busy time before the slow, winding down of nature into the deep sleep that winter brings. Two festivals, Lughnasad and the Autumn Equinox are celebrated this season – the bread and corn harvest, and the apple harvest, among others. It is a time when the light has turned towards the dark half of the year, and has that very special "slant" that gives everything a warm, autumnal glow. The days are still warm at the beginning of autumn, the nights gradually turning cooler until the first frosts appear to let us know that winter is on the way.

Autumn is a time of letting go. We take our inspiration from the natural world around us. Looking around we see the foliage dying back, the leaves changing colour and falling from the trees. Like the tree, we must learn to let go, for the leaf does not cling to the tree after its time has ended, nor does the tree cling to the leaf – they let go of each other and enjoy a new cycle of their lives. The tree turns inwards, to gather its energy throughout winter, and the leaf transforms into food for the tree, to supply it with the nourishment it needs to once again bud in the spring.

Think about what you need to let go of in your life during these three months. It could be bad habits, an attitude or possessions you don't need. It's a wonderful time to clear out the dross from your life in order to progress into winter, fully aware. Here are some examples, and things to think about:

1. Give your house a really good clear out. I do this every spring and autumn – starting with wardrobe. I donate to charity the clothes that I have not worn for a year. I take stock of what I need, and only of what I need, and restock accordingly (mostly from charity shops, however, underwear and socks I will buy new). I also go through books and all other possessions. If I haven't used them, or simply do not love them enough to keep them, then they too are donated to charity. Later in the season I wash down all the floors in my house – you can use a special mix of your favourite herbs and oils with vinegar and water to give them a really good scrubbing. I also use vinegar and water to wash all the windows in the house, dust all the blinds, and really get into all the nooks and crannies. Wood is bought and stored for the fireplace, and the oil tank is refilled. Once the house is fully prepared for winter, I can look forward to the time of Samhain; I know that I can sit back and begin to dream of new plans for the coming year.

2. Go apple picking. I used to do this as a child, and I loved it. It really connects you with the sounds, sights and smells of autumn. High in a ladder in a tree, with the wind playing in your hair, reaching for an apple, the scent of leaves all around you – it's an experience like no other.

3. Think about donating to a charity, if you do not already. Go over all your expenses, and see if there is anything left over that you could regularly donate to your chosen charity. If money is not an option, see about donating your time. This is very, very important to me – it is all too easy to forget that there are so many other living creatures out there that have hardships we could never even imagine.

4. Two festivals, mentioned previously, fall during the autumn season. Find out all that you can about each one – where they originated, what gods they might be dedicated to. See how it fits in with your own environment. I think it is important to incorporate your local festivals into the seasonal festivals of the pagan wheel of the year, so if your village has a fete at this time of year, talk to people about it, become a part of it. Learn the history of it. Celebrate the festivals in whatever way you see fit (for a ritual outline that you can use and adapt, please see Chapter 15). There are plenty of examples of seasonal rituals in books, and online (see suggested reading section at the end of this book).

The Ancestors of Place
This is a time of year to really deepen your connection with the ancestors of place. These are the people, flora and fauna of your local environment, who have all contributed to it simply by sharing that space that you now call home. In the autumn, when we are inspired by nature all around us, winding down and in the process of decay, of returning to the soil, we look to the ancestors of place.

Start with finding out about the local human history of your area. Begin recently and work your way back as far as you can. Find out the origins of your village, town or city's name. Find out about where you water comes from, where your food comes from. If you own a house, look into the history of the land upon which your house was built. Was something there before? I have deeds that go back hundreds of years for my house, and I can see that it was once farmland, then an orchard, then hovels were built upon it, and finally it sold at auction and the current houses were built. The spirits of all those who shared this land are still there – heard on the wind, felt deep within the earth. The old orchard is still there, deep in the ground, though the trees are long since gone. The people who inhabited the hovels – their blood, sweat and tears are a part of the land where I garden, give my offerings and meditate. There are songs and stories held within the land that are just waiting to be discovered.

Daily Prayers
Have you found some daily prayers through resources, or written your own? When do you pray? Is it at a certain time each day, or do you go more with the flow of events in the day? What is the nature of your first prayer of the day, and why?

Meditation
Have you begun to meditate? Have you managed at least 15 to 20 minutes a day? Have you had good days and bad days? What are some of your meditation experiences – are there any that stand out as particularly successful or unsuccessful? Keeping a daily meditation journal may help you to see progress, as well as help spot any difficult areas that may require more effort.

Inner Pathworking
Follow the steps in the previous section to meet with your spirit guide.

> *Your spirit guide stands before you. You bow, reverently. Your spirit guide then asks you the following questions – you answer them truthfully, and from the heart.*
> *"What causes you fear?"*
> *"What causes you pain?"*
> *"What destructive patterns in your life do you see and recognise?"*
> *"What is in your power to change?"*
> *Your spirit guide steps forwards, holding a chalice. The water inside this chalice has been moon-blessed. Your spirit guide dips a finger in the chalice, and draws a crescent moon on your forehead. You are then offered to drink from the chalice, and you do so, deeply. As the water flows into you, you find the inspiration and the awen to do*

the changes necessary in your life, should there be any. You say your thanks to your spirit guide, and watch as the figure slowly melts back into the mist.

Record what happened in a journal, if possible, so that you can go back and reflect upon this at a later date.

Outer Pathworking

Following the guidelines set out in the previous section, keep to your daily walks, noticing how the environment is changing around you. If possible, try to keep a journal to record the effects you can see around you – when the first birch leaves turned, when the apples from a certain type of tree came out, when the harvests came in. You can compare this to next year's cycle, to see if patterns emerge.

Altars

Have you created your altar? Does it change with the seasons, flowing in and out, or is it more permanent? Have you tended to your altar? Is there dust settling upon it, does it need attention?

Winter

The festivals that fall during the winter are Samhain and Yule. It is a time when the winds shift, blowing colder air and bringing with it rain, snow and sleet (at least in the UK). It is a time of great darkness, the light fading around 3.15pm and not emerging much before 8am in the mornings where I live. It is a difficult time for many, struggling to stick to a routine of work and family when all nature seems to be telling us is to take it a little easier now, to allow the darkness to let you sleep longer and dream deeper...

Winter is a time of apparent death, when a blanket of snow or frost covers the last traces of greenery that are still trying to survive despite the harsh conditions. It is a time of release into the cauldron of rebirth, to be allowed the time to manifest anew at Yule with the turning of the year and the turning of the wheel. However, rest must come first.

During the winter, we gather to ourselves, if we are lucky, friends and family in celebration during these two festivals. In between the busy time of these festivals we can take the time to withdraw, to recharge our batteries and find out what really matters to us, and then celebrate it in the darkest time of the year. It is not a time for standing defiant against the cycles of darkness in nature, but a time of celebrating them, honouring the darkness for the chance to rest and remembering the really important things in life.

Winter is the time for dreaming. We make plans for the coming year, and release the ideas that never came to light, or have been dead ends. We take the experience from the previous year and apply that to our new dreams, our new plans, and so go forth with perhaps a little more wisdom. Celebrate these transitions in ritual (see Chapter 15 for a ritual outline).

Winter is also the time for rediscovering the child within. Look at the world with the wonder of a child. Learn the processes of life and establish new boundaries, releasing the old ones. With the childlike awe of new discoveries, we can awaken once again to a world that may have been passing us by.

It is a good time for self-reflection, to understand how we act and react in different situations. We learn to act with intention and purpose, instead of reacting with unawareness. Examine your habits, how you are with different people and situations, when happy or when angered, when you are hurt or experience joy. See if you can alter these patterns into a weave that is more cohesive and beautiful in its design, beneficial to all.

Forgoing the sugar-induced insanity of Hallowe'en, at Samhain, we look instead into the darkness to see what it is that we fear. We face our own insanity by looking deep into the mirror of our soul through the long night. Leaving behind the commercialism that looms around Yule, we welcome the return of the light half of the year with new vision and clear hearts, awakening once again much as the sun is reborn.

In winter we must nurture our dreams close to our hearts, lest they collapse in the harshness of the biting wind. We dream deep and long, we dream and we scheme, in order to create a better world for all to be brought out into the light of the coming spring, with courage in our hearts and with joy in our souls.

Some things to do during these months are:

1. Go over or write up your Will. When you are gone, you will want to make it as easy as possible for those who remain to deal with your estate and your final wishes.
2. Visit the graves or other places of rest of your ancestors. Talk to them if you wish, or simply take in the beauty of the time and place, the cycles of nature flowing in and out...
3. Honour the time of the first frost. This is a special time in nature's calendar, when many things will be killed off by the cold.
4. Study all that you can about Druidry from other books. Research all that you can about the Celts, for it is from their worldview that Druidry began. Get a good foundation in history and archaeology during the cold months ahead. Use the time wisely.
5. Research all that you can on the festivals of winter mentioned above, and hold a ritual or celebration for each one (see Chapter 15 for more details).

The Ancestors of Blood

Our ancestors of blood are always with us. Whether we liked them or not, we are a part of them, holding genetic DNA, cultural attitudes and more. We may have come from a loving home, we may not even know who our biological parents are, having been adopted. There is never a barrier to connecting to the ancestors of blood, however, for they are right there, in your blood.

For some, this can be painful, especially if abuse or neglect have been involved. Yet it can also be a time of reconciliation, of understanding mistakes made and of releasing blame and finding healing. Instead we focus on what is important right now – that we simply be the best human beings that we can be.

If you are so inclined, look up your family tree in old parish records, or using online sources if a family tree has not already been created by a member of your family. However, always remember that there are so many strands to your family tree – that after you leave your great grandparents, the numbers begin to get astronomical in the amount of relatives you have, and following one strand is no more important than following another. Also remember that parish records can often leave out the female side, women marrying into families while their own is unacknowledged in the genealogy. We can become proud of an accomplished family member, yet disregard another all too easily. It is a time to honour all that has brought you to this place and time. If there are those in your life whom you simply are not willing to honour, then that too is fine – you can always come back to it if you so wish.

Remember always that your ancestors are not just people who lived hundreds of years previously. They begin with your parents, with all their love, faults, freckles and funny laughs. Honour them, if you can, for all that they are.

Daily Prayers

By now you will know if daily prayers are beneficial to your practice or not. I would recommend that if you have trouble remembering to pray daily, to still try to establish that connection as often as you can. Spontaneous prayers of thanks and gratitude, made from the heart, are just as good, if not better, than daily prayers that have been memorised by rote, and are not spoken with genuine feeling.

Meditation
Winter is a great time for deep meditation. The long, cold and dark winter months are all beneficial to a little time taken out for sitting and simply being in the present moment. Keep up the daily meditation as described previously, and allow yourself the time to go deeper, as the time and tide of the season allows.

Inner Pathworking
Follow the steps in the previous section to meet with your spirit guide.

> *Your spirit guide stands before you. You bow, reverently. Your spirit guide then asks you the following questions – you answer them truthfully, and from the heart.*
> *"How do you react when challenged by another, and how can you create peace instead of dissent?"*
> *"What patterns do you wish to alter?"*
> *"What dreams and aspirations do you hold that you never realised, but have the power to rethink now, and keep safe in order to bring to light in the spring?"*
> *"What is the face you wore before you were born?"* (A very powerful Zen koan.)
> *Your spirit guide steps forward with a heavy cloak, and bids you to sit down. You do so, and are wrapped in the cloak, covered in total darkness. You remain there – for minutes, hours, days – until at last you feel ready to shed the cloak, ready to face the light of the growing season and all that stands waiting in potential. With a cry, you cast off the cloak and spread your arms wide, welcoming the birth of new potential, and a certain fearlessness to see the light of day and the darkness of night. Your spirit guide smiles, and fades into the mist once again.*

Record what happened in a journal, if possible, so that you can go back and reflect upon this at a later date.

Outer Pathworking

As outlined in the previous section, keep to your daily walks, walking with light steps and leaving no trace but your energy lingering like a blessing. In winter, the earth sleeps, and so we walk softly, silently, honouring the silence around us. The birds do not sing as much, everything takes on the air of hushed quietude. We learn to move silently, ghosting through, noticing everything around us that is still alive, and that which has died. Even in the darkness or the harshness of a winter's storm, keep to the daily walks, for it is essential to understand your environment in all conditions.

Altars

Samhain is a great time for creating an altar dedicated to the ancestors of blood. Yule is also a wonderful time to create a personal altar for your Druid work, if you have not done so already. Decorating it with boughs of evergreen, photos of loved ones and all that you hold sacred can inspire you through the long winter months. Keep the altar well tended, and regularly use it for your meditations and prayers.

Spring

The first signs of spring are appearing, though it may yet be some time before the snow melts in some places. The days are getting longer as the sun rises and sets further apart along the horizon. The festivals celebrated during the spring tide are Imbolc and the Spring Equinox. It is a time when hopes are renewed for the coming year, and the dreams that we held close during the long winter months can start to become a reality.

Spring is a time of action. Yet we must still guard the seeds that we have held all winter, and ensure that we do not sow them too early, for they may be killed by late frosts. Whether these seeds are physical flora or the seeds of our intention, the timing remains the same. We must gauge when it is best to plant, and to do so we must be aware of the world around us.

Spring was also the hungry time for our ancestors – when food was the most scarce, after the winter stores have been depleted and the first crops and foraging foods not yet available. It is a time to be thankful for all that you have, and to ensure that your community is kept safe and strong.

It is also a season of renewal – now is the time when we can see the first shoots appearing through the leaf mould, the buds swelling and bursting on the trees, the first lambs bouncing in the fields. We can take inspiration from this renewal, and use it to enrich our lives and the lives of others around us.

Think about the seeds that you have held close during the long winter nights, those dreams and intentions just waiting for the sun and warmth to blossom into a new cycle. Here are some things to do during the spring months:

1. Spring cleaning. As in autumn, really give the house a thorough cleaning.
2. Keep a record, if you haven't already during your outer pathworking, of the time when the first snowdrops, daffodils and lambs appeared, or whatever signals spring where you live.
3. Watch the sun rise and set further along the horizon each day – notice the time of year when it really seems to jump!
4. Do some work for your community. It doesn't matter which community, whether it is the community of heathland that needs a litter clear-up, or your local community centre that is having a bake sale to raise funds for charity – now is the time to pull together in whatever sense you are able to. Strengthening the bonds of community, helping others and having compassion for the world are essential to living an honourable life.
5. Research all that you can on the festivals of spring mentioned above, and hold a ritual or celebration for each

one (see Chapter 15 for more details).

6. Donate some food from your weekly shop at your supermarket, if you shop at one and it has a collection bin. If you shop more locally, find the nearest shelter and see if you can donate any food or money to help people through the spring months.

The Ancestors of Tradition

Spring is the perfect time to take inspiration from our ancestors of tradition. With autumn and winter we delved into the ancestors of place and also those of our own bloodlines. In spring, we regard those spiritual ancestors who we look up to, who help to shape our thinking and our worldview. These may be guides and teachers of our present time – they may also be those of ancient times. Though we cannot know what Druids thought or did for certain at any point in history, we can still investigate that which piques our interest, that which gives us the inspiration to continue on our journey. If we, for example, want to look into possible ancestors of tradition within the Iron Age culture, we would first have to research that historical time to inform our views. If you have not done this already through winter, now is the time to begin.

We might also take inspiration from stories and myths to honour the ancestors of tradition. Great heroes from folktales, epic myth cycles and legends are all great places to look for the awen, from the Arthurian legends to the Welsh Mabinogion. Delve deeply into your Druidry at this stage, and find out where your inspiration to be a Druid comes from. Look closely at your guides and mentors. Find out their stories, and honour them for helping you on your chosen spiritual path. A good place to start is by reading Ronald Hutton's *Blood and Mistletoe* – it's not for the faint hearted, but it's the best historical account of Druidry to date that I have come across.

Daily Prayers

How have your daily prayers developed? Do you feel a stronger connection to that which you are establishing a relationship with, whether it is the deities, the ancestors, or the spirits of place? Do you enjoy your daily prayers, or are they becoming a chore? Are you being consistent, or do you enjoy an impromptu prayer as the sun sets, or when you see the moon high in the sky, or the thunderclouds of spring approaching? Have you tried both daily and impromptu prayers?

Meditation

Now that the days are warming up, if you have been meditating inside, it is time to take it outside. Again, with the exact same awareness, it is simply a time to breathe, to listen to the world around you, to be 100% in the moment. If the meditation sessions have been going well, and have been beneficial, see about possibly having two sessions a day – perhaps morning and evening, of around 15 to 20 minutes.

Inner Pathworking

Follow the steps in the previous section to meet with your spirit guide.

> *Your spirit guide stands before you. You bow, reverently. Your spirit guide then asks you the following questions – you answer them truthfully, and from the heart.*
> *"What brings you joy?"*
> *"Is there a difference between the person you are inside and the outer manifestation?"*
> *"What is it that you can do now, to be the person that you wish to be, and can become?"*
> *"Do you truly wish to break free of any negative patterns?"*
> *"What is that you will plant this season, what dreams will you manifest this spring and how will you do it?"*

Your spirit guide leads you around the spiral path to the top of the Tor in the light of pre-dawn. As you stand at the summit, you feel the energies of land, sea and sky all around you. You turn to face the sunrise, waiting. You can feel the anticipation of the dawn in everything around you. Slowly the light begins to grow and you feel the corresponding energy within you rise. Finally the sun breaks over the horizon and washes over you. You feel the waves of light and energy flow through you and you are fully aware of the cycle of life. Day follows night, light follows dark. You are aware of yourself within that cycle.

Record what happened in a journal, if possible, so that you can go back and reflect upon this at a later date.

Outer Pathworking
Following the guidelines set out in the previous section, keep to your daily walks, noticing how the environment is changing around you. If possible, try to keep a journal to record the effects you can see around you – when the first nettles appear, when the snows receded and the ground first showed through; the first crocus. Record the time if and when you see a farmer ploughing his field. Note down the time of day of the sunset and sunrise, if you can – and try to witness these before, after or during your walks.

Altars
With the warming months ahead, find a time when it is suitable to build an altar outside, if you can. You will have now become familiar with your indoor altar – how will an outdoor one be different? Tend to both, if you wish, or simply move the indoor one outside. Notice how it feels to meditate or pray outside, if you have been performing these daily routines indoors.

Summer

Summer is a time of high energy. It can be a glorious time for those who are comfortable with the energies of light and sun. For those who are sensitive it can be a testing time, when everyone around them seems to be buzzing and all they want to do is hide in the cool, dark shade. Either way, working with the energies of the season as opposed to fighting the currents is always the preferable route and can be done to suit all sensibilities. Two festivals, Beltane and the Summer Solstice, mark this tide.

In the full light of the sun there is nowhere to hide. It is a good time to focus on acceptance of reality and also of personal responsibility. In this tide of high energy, we must be extra aware of how our actions affect the world at large.

Reality is a slippery little devil. Our minds are so adept at creating our own version of reality that the boundaries between what is real and what is not can become so blurred as to be indistinguishable.

Our thoughts can control us so much that they can keep us running around in circles, spinning off into the depths of our minds and in doing so, we miss out on all the wonders of the present moment. Most people don't enjoy being in the present moment – they avoid it at all costs. However, this is because they have probably, for the most part, never truly experienced being in the present moment. Problems arise when our perceptions of reality become twisted with the imaginative and creative thought processes that our human brains are so capable of.

We can sometimes act dishonourably – sometimes it is to justify certain behaviour, or to explain events. The key is to become aware of it when you are doing it, to stop and say, "Right. I know what the facts are, and I'm going to stick to them, and not change them to suit my own desires."

We are responsible for our own actions and we all must be the best human beings we can at this present moment. Actions have consequences. However, we must also be aware and have some compassion for those who are caught up in their own realities, to a certain extent. We don't have to live in them, or even partake of that reality, but we can try to understand the reasons why.

We have to learn how to live in the here and now. Being alive and present allows no time for emotional attachment to our thoughts and feelings – we still respond emotionally to situations, but we don't become attached to the emotion itself.

Let us continue to tell stories, but not make up the story of our own life. Our own lives are brilliant and fascinating enough – we don't need to add more drama to them. By doing so, we will miss our own lives, living instead in our minds and forgoing some of the wondrous nature that is constantly unfolding right before our very eyes. We can hurt other people by making up stories to suit our egos and our needs, and the person we hurt most is ourselves. Reality is not such a bad place. Here are some things to do during the summer months:

1. Stand in the full face of the sun and acknowledge the reality of who you are.
2. Take some time in ritual to learn your story, the stories of the land and the ancestors.
3. Learn all you can about the two festivals that fall during this tide and create rituals for them (for more information, please see Chapter 15).
4. Celebrate and recite your story, the story of the land and the story of the ancestors in the full light of the sun.
5. Make a personal commitment to take care of your physical body as well as your mental health – now is the perfect time to eat fresh, healthy food and to start a balanced wellness regime.

The Ancestors of the Future
By now you will have worked with the ancestors of blood, place and tradition. It is important to maintain your work with the

ancestors, for we must understand our past in order to find our place in the present and also to work with our future ancestors.

As stated above, all our actions have consequences. In always remembering the ancestors of the future, it can help us to moderate our behaviour and actions so that we will have the most positive impact we can upon the world. Even if we do not have children of our own, there will be children in the world who will inherit our legacy and it is for them and their descendants that we must consider every decision we make.

We recycle not in order to get good "karma" points or green credentials – we do so because of our ancestors of the future. We invest in ethical companies for our ancestors of the future. We look at what we purchase, how every penny spent is a vote as to how the present will become the future. We must take a long, hard look at our ethics and decide how we can change ourselves, thereby influencing the planet. It is not enough to say that one individual cannot make a change – if everyone thought of the future ancestors, even just a little, the world would be a much better place.

Daily Prayers

Really consider what it is that you are praying to, or praying for. Examine how often you offer a prayer of thanksgiving as opposed to a prayer of request for aid. Think about the flow of prayer, the relationship that you are creating with that which you are praying to. Is it a little one-sided? On whose part? Prayer is a form of exchange that should flow in beautiful spirals, inwards and outwards to open the self, soul to soul. How can you improve on that relationship in order to achieve a deep and meaningful prayerful attitude? What does it mean to you to have a prayerful attitude?

Meditation

If the weather has been kind, or even if it has not, we have begun to meditate out of doors as much as possible. How have these sessions been going? Have you managed to meditate for longer periods of time, or is the outdoors too distracting? If you find yourself distracted outside at this time of high energy, why not try a walking meditation? You can even do this during your outer pathworking sessions, as long as you are able to focus on breathing and concentrate on walking mindfully, not becoming absorbed in what you are seeing around you. Paying attention to everything is key – it's very simple and equally very difficult.

Inner Pathworking
Follow the steps in the previous section to meet with your spirit guide.

> *Your spirit guide stands before you. You bow, reverently. Your spirit guide then asks you the following questions – you answer them truthfully, and from the heart.*
> *"How are you currently living to your full potential?"*
> *"What gives you strength and what depletes your energy? Is this relationship honourable?"*
> *"How accepting are you of your responsibilities? Of your previous actions?"*
> *"What can you do to make the world a better place?"*
> *"What does it mean to live in service?"*
> *"What is honour?"*
> *Your guide draws the symbol of awen on the ground before you, the three rays emanating from the drops that issued from the cauldron of transformation. You are asked to meditate upon what awen means to you and how you can inspire others in their journey. Taking awen and honour together, you are asked to carry these both into the wider world. Will you accept?*

Record your finding in a journal if possible.

Outer Pathworking
The days are long now – evening walks can be glorious when the

heat of the day has cooled off. Early morning walks are ideal too – watching the sun rise if you are a morning person (if not, I suggest watching the sun rise during the winter months, as it rises much later in the morning). Notice how the air changes during the day, from the smells and sounds of the intense noon to the softer energies of twilight or pre-dawn. What birds are singing around you? What animals are revelling in the increased light?

Altars

You have hopefully been spending time at your outdoor altar, perhaps in meditation or in giving offerings to the spirits of place. Does your altar change with the seasons, or does it remain a steadfast marker point in the wheel of the year? Try to meditate at your outdoor altar if possible, or even spend the night outside, perhaps in meditation or prayer in the warmer evenings. Sleeping out of doors is a wonderful experience and what better way to commune with nature than spending a night out using your altar as a focal point? If this is not possible, consider making a trip out to the countryside where you can create a temporary altar to perform the same task – remember that you should leave nothing behind except that which will biodegrade and which will not harm the environment in any way.

Chapter Thirteen

Craft Names

Within Druidry, and indeed in modern paganism, it is not unusual to adopt a craft name within your tradition. It is not necessary, and if you feel that you don't need one, or one doesn't appeal, then by all means forgo the craft name. However, choosing a craft name can enhance your connection to your tradition.

Craft names can provide an air of mystery and magic. We can choose something that reflects our work, such as Oak Seeker, Coll (hazel, if working with ogham), or Pathfinder. We can choose something that reflects a part of the environment that we love – Alder, Willow, Rain. We can put two words together that express a deep part of our soul, or a deep love that we have, such as Gentle Bear, Running Horse, or Autumn Song (my craft name). We can adopt names of the gods and goddesses that we love, such as Nehalennia, Freya, Lugh, Branwen, Rhiannon or Bridget. There are also mythological names like Merlin, Morgan and Nimue that might strike a chord deep within our hearts. We can even choose names from fantasy books that we love – Gandalf, Radagast, Arwen, Goldberry, Eomer, Eowyn or Faramir (all *Lord of the Rings* names). What matters most is that our name expresses a deep part of our soul; that when we utter it, write it, exhale it into the twilight it means something to us, connects us to the awen.

You can inscribe your craft name upon your altar, or your tools. You can sign correspondence with it. You may even change your name to your craft name if you feel that better reflects who you are. I like having both names, as I can honour my two grand-mothers for whom I am named after, and honour my tradition with my craft name.

We might choose our craft name, or we might be gifted it by

another. We could meditate, commune with the local spirits of place, or deity, and ask that they bestow us a name. In some magical traditions, a craft name is given upon initiation into the tradition, or upon completion of various grades. When working alone, we do not have to wait to have a name bestowed upon us – we can seek it out ourselves from whatever inspires us whenever we feel ready. We can ask our ancestors, our spirit guides, even our friends and family for ideas and inspiration.

Our craft names may also change with time. As we grow and develop in our spirituality we might find that we outgrow our name, and thereby be inspired to choose another that better suits our current work. We can include our naming in ceremonies, whether it is our first time or our fifth time in choosing a craft name. Taking on a name is not something to be done lightly, however – it requires much thought and meditation if you wish for it to be important to your work.

Whatever name you choose, or however you decide to be named, honour that name with all that you are. Find ways of being that reflect your name in deep and compassionate ways, working to create peace and harmony in your life and in all life around you.

Section Three

Creating Your Own Path

In this section we will look at how we can create our own personal Druid rituals, as well as our own daily practice. I offer guidelines and suggestions – as a solitary you are free to use them, be inspired, or seek your own way down the forest path. All that matters is that you walk your own path, for no one else can do it for you.

Chapter Fourteen

Designing Druid Ritual

Druid ritual is about connection and relationship – it is a way of experiencing a moment, of taking the time to stop and honour the sacredness of the time and place. We learn more and more that we can honour the sacredness of each and every moment, living in awareness as much as we can. As with meditation, ritual is about deliberately taking time out to simply be in the moment. With Druidry, it is all about the intention behind the action in ritual and in everyday life that makes it truly special.

Druid rituals honour the seasons, and generally follow the eight festivals that are based on the cycles of the sun, agriculture and the seasons, the wheel of the year and life markers/passages. They also follow the lunar cycles, the tides, sunrise and sunset, moonrise and moonset. They are held for significant markers in one's life – weddings, funerals, births, divorce, coming of age and so on. Equally, Druid ritual can simply be taking time out to reconnect with oneself and the world around – the natural environment – at any given point in time.

Ritual can be elaborate, written in advance, enacting the drama of the moment. It can also be spontaneous; pulling the car over as you see the full moon rise over the heathland. What matters is that the time is taken to perform/participate in it. Our intention is all important.

Is ritual important? Many Druids perform ritual on a fairly regular basis – at least the seasonal rituals that celebrate the turning of the wheel of the year. Many also honour the phases of the moon, in whatever aspect, whether it be quarter, half, full or new. There are also some for whom daily ritual gives special meaning to their lives and their loves – the rising or setting of the sun and moon, for instance, or saying a prayer of thanksgiving or a blessing before partaking of food and drink. But is it all that important?

The answer to this will be based on our personal relationship to the natural world around us. For some, daily ritual helps them to connect with the rhythms of life that might not otherwise be apparent. If you are living in the city, it may be hard to hear the blackbirds singing at dusk above the din of rush-hour traffic, or you may not be able to see the sun or moon rise due to buildings blocking your view. Ritual can help us remember the natural world around us, even when we feel distanced from it (though we are never separated). For others a daily ritual isn't that important, for they already feel much more connected simply in their living circumstances. It's akin to a friendship, in a sense – sometimes your friend lives far away, and you have to make a special effort to keep in contact with her. Sometimes your friend lives right next door, and it's much easier to keep in touch.

Druid ritual can do the same for us, keeping us connected to our spirituality, whatever our circumstances. Too easily we can become lost in our own worlds, realities that we have created out of our emotions and thoughts. Ritual can say, "Hey, look – enough. Stop. Look at what's really going on around you. Hear the stag calling. Hear the aeroplane. Watch the sun rise. Notice the change in the seasons. The world is more than just you."

With Druid ritual, we gain inspiration from the natural world around us. That is what awen is – an insight into nature: the nature of the world around us and our own human nature in turn. By doing Druid ritual we take the time to pause, to reflect and to take in inspiration so that we may exhale it with love and compassion back into the world. We become the inspiration, the awen.

So, is ritual important? I think so. Even if we use the friend analogy, ritual keeps us from taking things for granted. It brings awareness and magic back into our mundane lives no matter what our circumstances are. No matter where we are in life, taking a moment to stop and simply be in the moment can help us gain inspiration and insight, and to also give back with thanks for all the blessings that we have received.

It is so easy to lose the sense of magic in everyday life. We had it, perhaps, as children – our imaginations not yet restricted by what was normal, or appropriate, or social/cultural dictates. Ritual helps us to rediscover that magic, to pause and to breathe, to allow our soul to expand as well as our minds, and especially to rediscover that sense of wonderment that we may have left behind as we have grown older. The world is a fascinating place – ritual helps us to remember that. A woodland ritual will make us see the mystique and magic that lies in the nemeton of the forest, allowing us into that sacred space for a short time to dance with the energy of the trees, the dryads and the forest dwellers.

Ritual allows time for our souls to grow, to expand, to drink in all that the awen, inspiration and the world have to offer. Ritual also provides us a time, space and framework in which to experience that ultimate freedom. Ritual is magic itself, transforming us, altering our worldview and affecting us on a soul level like nothing else.

Creating Your Own Druid Ritual

Here is a ritual outline that I use for longer, more elaborate rituals. For impromptu rituals or daily rituals it is much shorter, consisting of words spoken in the brilliance of the moment, and gestures that have been used daily, such as bowing, holding the hands in prayer position or other mudras (traditionally Eastern meditation positions, but I have also created my own).

The Guardians
Here I ask the guardian spirits of the place for their permission to work my ritual in their domain.

Hail Guardian Spirits of this place! I have come here in peace and with clear intent. I have come here to (name reason for ritual). I ask, with respect, that you accept my presence. Hail Guardian Spirits of this place!

It is important to wait to hear for the response before continuing. They may not want us in their area at that particular moment, or our intention may not be clear. A response may come in the form of hearing words, or a feeling of calm and acceptance from within, or a soft breeze caressing your cheek; the song of a blackbird.

Set-Up
The altar is set up, food is laid out and the fire/candles lit. Incense may be offered and music played softly if indoors – outdoors I prefer to listen to the songs of nature. The circle can be laid out using the nearby natural resources, whether it be stones, twigs, leaves, etc.

The Call for Peace
The Call for Peace is a traditional Druid way of establishing peace in the ritual – it is a form of prayer.

May there be peace in the North! May there be peace in the South! May there be peace in the West! May there be peace in the East! I call for peace in my heart and mind, for the world around me and towards all fellow beings.

The Circle Casting
The circle is cast using whatever method you prefer.

Sacred Ones, spirit of the beech that stands before me, spirits of the valley that surrounds me, dryads and devas, all you who have heard my intention, I ask that you join with me in my sacred ritual. Soul to soul and spirit to spirit, may we commune together in a harmonious union and in honour of all that is sacred.

I give of my energy to this circle, mingling and communing with those of the spirits of nature to create a sanctuary of peace.

(Energy is pushed out from your hand/wand/staff, to blend with and strengthen the circle.)

I am honoured to be in this sacred time and in this sacred place. I honour the earth below me, the sky above me and the seas that surround me. The spirits of the three worlds of land, sea and sky flow through me, and I am a part of the greater song. May I sing it with clear intention and harmony, honouring all beings, the gods and the ancestors.

Consecration

If you wish to consecrate your circle or the ritual space, you may do so with water, incense, burning sage, a candle's flame – whatever fits in with your needs and ritual design. You may do something similar to the following:

With incense I consecrate this sacred space, offering it in remembrance that it is always holy. There is no unsacred place, and with the smoke from these herbs and resins I honour this time and this place with all that I am.

With water I consecrate this sacred space, offering it in remembrance that it is always holy. The waters of the world are sacred, and this water I offer with my blessings that all water be held sacred.

Honouring the Quarters

You can now choose to honour the quarters if you so wish – remember that you are not commanding them to be present, for they are always there. You are simply opening your awareness to them. You can say these or similar words:

I honour the Spirit of the North, the Earth Mother, the Great Bear.
I honour the Spirit of the East, the Sky Father, the Great Eagle.
I honour the Spirit of the South, the Fire Brother, the Great Dragon.
I honour the Spirit of the West, the Rain Sister, the Great Whale.

The Three Worlds

Take a moment to reflect upon the three worlds of land, sea and sky, traditional to the Druid/Celtic worldview. Feel the land within you, the sea around you and the sky above you. Equally, feel each realm within you. In concentric circles around you, you can open your awareness to the land, sea and sky, seeing where you fit in the great cycle.

I honour the realms of the three worlds, of land, sea and sky, with all that I am. I hold their energy within me even as I see them ever present around me. May I be blessed by the three worlds, and may I serve them well.

The Ancestors

I call to the ancestors of place, blood and tradition to be with me in my sacred rite. To the ancestors whose tears and blood, joy and happiness have been felt upon this land, whose songs course through my blood, and whose spirit lives on through my celebrations, I call to you and open my awareness of you within my sacred rite.

Invocation of Deity (whether particular or generic)

I call upon my Lady of the Stars and Moon
To the Bringer of dreams and twilight
I call upon my Lady of the Loom
The Weaver of fates in the night
I call upon the Lady of the Lake
The Singer of the Evensong

I call upon my beloved Goddess
May she be forever strong

I call upon the Lord of the Sun
The Rider in the sky
I call upon the Lord of the Winds
To the Eagle as he flies
I call upon the King Stag
To the son, lover and sacrifice
I call upon the Lord of the Wildwood
Laughing, free and wise

Note: again, this is simply an opening of personal awareness of deity – we are not commanding or summoning them to our ritual, for they are always there.

The Declaration
This is where we declare our intention to the spirits of place, the ancestors, the gods and all nature. It is also a chance to refine our personal intention, to solidify it within our souls.

I come here to celebrate Beltane, the abundance and fertility of nature that surrounds me. The fires of passion burn strong in the warm sunshine, and all nature turns to thoughts of love. I celebrate the greening of the leaves, the mating calls of birds, the birthing of wild animals. When the world seems washed afresh and anew with life, I honour it with all that I am.

The Ritual Act
This can be an act performed in honour of the time; the reason that you are come to ritual. It is symbolic – the braiding of coloured ribbons to signify the joining together of souls to create something new; a song or dance performed in celebration; words spoken in honour of the season; sacrifice given.

Note: there is no blood sacrifice in modern Druidry; we sacrifice something that cannot be replaced – a treasured object, for instance. It must have a very special meaning to you, and be symbolic and meaningful.

The Feast and Offering
The food and drink or offering are blessed.

> *May the Goddess and God and the spirits of this land bless this offering and accept it, freely given with honour and respect.*

Or:

> *Goddess, bountiful Earth Mother, bless this bread/offering and suffuse it with your love.*
> *God, powerful Sky Father, bless this mead/offering and may it lend strength to all.*

The drink/offering is held high above the head.

> *Thanks be to the land!*

A sip is taken from the cup and a libation poured onto the ground.
The bread/offering is held out before.

> *Thanks be to the land!*

A bit of bread is eaten, and a measure of bread is then laid out in offering.

> *Please accept these gifts given with joy – as we take, so too do we freely give.*

A full feast/meal can then be eaten if so desired, with any remnants shared with the spirits of place.

When the feasting/offering is done, you may offer gifts of poetry and storytelling, dance or painting – sharing the awen of the season with nature. This is traditionally known as the "eisteddfod", performed in group celebrations. There is no reason why solitaries cannot incorporate this into their rituals and share it with the spirits of the land, the ancestors and the gods should they so wish.

The rite is then nearing its end. Honour and respect are paid to the deities, to the spirits of land, sea and sky, to the ancestors, the four quarters and to the spirits of place using words similar to that which opened your awareness to them.

Closing the Circle
Stand in the centre and feel the circle around you, a symbol of the greater cycle. Know that you are a part of that cycle always. Draw the energy of the circle back into your body in a similar manner to which it was cast. Thank the spirits of place, the dryads and devas and all others who have shared your intention.

I give my thanks to those who have been with me in my sacred rite. I ask that the circle be released so that its blessings may spread into the wider world.

The Closing

May the Spirits of this Place be nourished as much as their presence has nourished my own soul. Guardian Spirit, I give you my heartfelt thanks. This ritual ends in peace as it began. May the blessings I have received go with me as I depart this place, to nourish, strengthen and sustain me throughout the days and nights, the turning of the seasons and the Great Cycle of Life. May awen and peace flow through me and the world. So may it be!

Chapter Fifteen

Daily Practice

How can we incorporate more spirituality into our everyday lives? By truly living our religion, our spirituality and our calling.

A religion or spirituality cannot be read about, or simply thought about – it must be experienced. Like life, it is the *doing* that counts. Yes, we must think – carefully and deeply, about what we do as human beings. We must also act upon that thinking with full awareness, otherwise the opportunity to really live slips us by.

There are so many ways in which we can bring more awareness and more spirituality into our daily routines. For instance, a prayer upon awakening is a brilliant way to start the day. Whether you believe in the gods, or spirits of place, the ancestors or all of the former is a matter for your own path. But coming to an awareness of them physically and emotionally – through living your meditations, prayers, rituals and devotions – can make all the difference.

After prayer upon awakening, we then get up and perform our ablutions, already aware of the sanctity of life. We can say a prayer of thanks to the goddess of the waters, the local water source, to the oceans of the world as we run the tap to wash our face. We create an awareness of the spirit and sanctity of water.

When we make our breakfast, or pour a cup of tea, we give thanks to gods, the spirits, to the earth for her abundance. We take time to acknowledge where our food and drink come from, and in that acknowledgement continue our day in a sacred manner. We are establishing a strong relationship with the world around us by doing so.

We can say a prayer or chant a charm when we are about to drive our car somewhere. Equally, we can say a prayer of thanks for hearing the blackbird's song of spring, or upon seeing the sunshine after months of rain. Seeing the moon, or a particular constellation in the sky, can evoke spontaneous prayers, said either aloud or in the mind. Prayers to the rising and setting sun, to the rising and setting moon can be said, as well as prayers before bed. Even getting into the bathtub can become spiritual, with words honouring clean, hot water, and/or a pentagram, awen or any other symbol that is meaningful to you drawn on the water's surface to acknowledge the sacredness. Gardening, working with others, playing with children – these can all be sacred times as well.

Certain times of day might be better for taking time apart for those who prefer a stricter routine. A set time in the morning, noon, afternoon or evening might be more suitable – it is all about personal choice.

We can use short rituals as well as prayer – a bow to the sun or moon, the lighting of a candle upon awakening, offering of incense or food at the beginning or end of each day. Daily offerings of food from one's plate are a great way to connect with the land and your immediate environment. Offerings of song and poetry, artistic work, dance and movement – all these can be incorporated into daily rituals to further establish your relationship with place, deity and the ancestors. Taking the time is what is most important – taking the time to connect with the spiritual world around you. We are never alone; we cannot be separate. We all live together on this planet side by side. Seeing this connection is pure awen.

Daily meditation is very good for grounding and centring, for considering the self and the wider world and finding our place within it. Taking a few moments of stillness and silence to contemplate the day, the self, or just to breathe can work wonders. Regular daily practice of sitting meditation carries through into other aspects of our lives, where we bring awareness into everything, and in doing so take away the illusionary drama and see reality for the wondrous gift that it is. It requires discipline, however, to sit through the boredom, to sit when we don't feel like it, to be aware when we'd rather be daydreaming. Yet this discipline is, as I have found out, necessary for clarity.

Create songs for the sunrise, or write new chants for the full moon. Sing something improvisational when you see the first blackthorn in flower, or raise your arms to honour the sun dog's myriad colours in the sky. The key is to just do it. Make everything sacred. The secular world may try to make us feel silly about doing so – but just try it. You may just find that your soul opens in response.

Chapter Sixteen

Walking Your Own Path

Venturing out on your own spiritual path can be daunting at first. You may not know where to turn; the path may become obscured with doubt. What matters most is that you walk it with integrity and honour, being true to yourself and bringing forth an awareness of the sacredness of all things and the cycles of life.

This book only offers an introduction to walking the path of Druidry – there is much more to be discovered. Read everything that you can on the Druids, on Celtic religion and from historical texts. Meld this research with experiential learning – you can only truly learn by doing. Modern Druidry has no set liturgy, for its roots stem from an oral tradition that was lost to the mists of time. People have gathered what fragments they could from history and archaeology, stories and myths, fashioning them into a spirituality that makes sense to them and which honours the world around them. You too can do this of your own accord – all it takes is a little effort and dedication to the task. You must be willing to learn. You must also be willing to understand that no one knows everything, and that it is up to you to ask the questions and, when answers cannot be found from others, find your own.

You may find it lonely at times, walking the path of awen in solitude. You may also love the solitude and the freedom that it offers. There is nothing stopping you from corresponding with others on the path – there are plenty of organisations and moots that can help you to connect with like-minded people, without becoming indoctrinated into something that may feel too rigid for your personal needs. Indeed, on your path to learning you most certainly will come into contact with others who are also on the search.

For some the solitary path comes easily. These are people who find the utmost sanctity in the world where there are the least amount of distractions. These are also people who are content with their own company. Whether out of choice or due to other circumstances such as geographical location, one must learn to rely on one's own wits and to develop an awareness of the self, which can only be found in solitude. When we are at ease with our own self, we can then be more at ease with others.

Social media and other forms of communication make getting in touch with others so very easy these days, as long as there is electricity to supply the different gadgets. Yet we can become far too reliant on these forms of communication, using it to avoid spending time with ourselves and with nature; they can be far too distracting and entice us away from the very important task of learning how to simply be in one's own company.

Time spent alone is precious time to look within, to check on our self and see if everything is okay. Not enough time is spent doing this, in my opinion. Giving this gift of attention to ourselves, we can see where we are simply reacting to events, instead of acting with intention. It gives us a chance to be compassionate with ourselves, and thereby allowing us to be more compassionate with others. We check in on others all the time with social media – what I suggest is that we check in with ourselves as well.

There is a marked increase in the number of people who follow a Druid path and, indeed, all pagan paths. In today's society, we can become so distanced from nature that we feel we need to do something to return to it; something that will connect us once again with the rhythms and flows of life. However, this separation is in itself an illusion that we have created, for we can never be separate as long as we are living and breathing in this world. By the mere fact of our existence, by the breath that we share with all other beings on this planet, we have a shared existence and a shared experience. We are never disconnected;

we are never truly alone.

The illusion can be very convincing though. It is supported with lifestyles and gadgets that seem to help fund the energy of the illusion. We commute to work on a train with hundreds of people and feel lonely, as everyone is reading a paper, on their phones or listening to their music, shutting out everyone else. For some highly sensitive individuals, this is even a self-preservation technique. We have mobile phones that can connect us with thousands of people anytime, anywhere and yet we have very little human interaction with most of them. We live in smaller and smaller family units where interaction with grandparents, cousins, aunts and uncles is ever decreasing for whatever reason – time, distance, etc.

Paganism, and Druidry in particular, can serve to address this need to reconnect, illusion or no. With so many technological advances, someone might be drawn to Druidry to get away from their machines, the hum of electricity and the constant noise, in an attempt to return to the natural cycles that are reflected in our environment. Some may be called by reading the poetry of the Romantics, or through historical interests or self-actualization. Some may be following their blood lineage, Celtic or otherwise. Others might feel called by the land upon which they live and use Druidry as the language with which to communicate.

More and more, people are choosing to follow a nature-based spirituality. Their reasons may be legion, but love of nature is at the very heart. For me, to be a Druid means not only a love of nature, but service to nature, to the world. We cannot take with abandon – we must give back. We must work hard to protect the things we love from our ever increasingly materialistic society. Its rampant technological advances often do not take into consideration the impact on the rest of the world. We look at our impact on the world, examining it closely to see if we are living in harmony. It is about seeing the sanctity and the sacredness in all things, using the language of Druidry to help us relate.

Druidry is all about the bigger picture. It is about our legacy and what we will leave to our ancestors of the future. It is learning from the past and living fully in the present, mindful of how we live and how we love. It is an ever evolving tradition that works with the talent and energy of the individual in service to the whole.

With the rise of numbers in Druidry, we need to remember this service to the world. It is not only something for us, but something for the entire planet. We not only practice Druidry for ourselves, but for the benefit of all. This is not altruistic, merely an outcome of service to the land. In service we grow in ourselves. We must look deep within to find the reasons for our Druidry, taking a long hard look at ourselves. We must also remember to look outside ourselves to the world at large.

Druidry can be summed up in three words – truth, honour and service. Yet these words can be very vague – what do they really mean to those on the Druid path?

Truth is not just figurative and literal truth. There are other dimensions to the word when we see it in accordance with our views of the world and religion or spirituality. Druids live in reverence of nature, connecting to the world through awen, the flowing inspiration that guides and directs; the soul song. When each thing is living in accordance to its own soul song, in accordance to its own nature, then it is following its own truth.

The world around us tries to muddy the waters of our truth, making us believe we need more than we could possibly know what to do with, making us think we are above others, making us feel inferior, unworthy and unloved. It tries to tell us that we are lacking. When we take a step back away from the world, we can examine it from a different perspective, seeing what is often termed in Druidry as "the truth against the world".

This truth is our soul song. It shines from us when we live in accordance with nature. It flows like the awen when we care for others and the planet. It springs forth when we acknowledge the times and tides of life and death. When we step away from what really matters, from living our own truth, we can feel distanced from the world and from each other, and perhaps even our own selves. We must return to the basics of where our place is within nature, and how we can live in harmony and balance with it. When we do, we are then living our truth.

Honour is another word that lies in the hazy mists of time. It has connotations of chivalry, fealty and nobility. Yet honour is simply the courage to live our soul truth in the world. It is standing strong by our principles of balance and harmony, making the world a better place for all. Returning again to what really matters, to our place in the world, is at the heart of honour. It is not a one-time thing that we can achieve and then sit back, resting on our laurels. Honour requires hard work, all the time, to see that we are indeed living our soul truths to the best of our ability.

When we come to understand truth and honour, the natural outcome is service. We live our lives in service to our Druidry – we can do no other. We are not subservient to anyone but ourselves. Living in accordance to our own nature, our own truths and finding sustainability through honour, it naturally results in service to the world – that same world that tries to rail against our truth! The cycle is ever flowing, and we work in service to the truth and the world in equal measure. That is where we find the most balance and harmony.

With that in mind, we take a deep breath and simply get started on our own life path. No one can walk it for us. We live our soul truths in honour within the world. We are fully aware of the great spiralling dance, seeing ourselves within it, represented by the seasons, the tides and the life cycles of everything around us. We live in service to that great cycle. It is awen. It is courage. It is Druidry.

May your path be blessed with inspiration.

Bibliography

Carr-Gomm, P. (2002) *Druid Mysteries: Ancient Wisdom for the 21st Century*, Rider

Chadwick, N. (2002) *The Celts*, Folio Society

Green, M. J. (2005) *Exploring the World of the Druids*, Thames and Hudson Ltd

Hutton, R. (2011) *Blood and Mistletoe: The History of the Druids in Britain*, Yale University Press

Hutton, R. (1999) *The Triumph of the Moon: A History of Modern Pagan Witchcraft*, Oxford Paperbacks

Restall Orr, E. (2004) *Living Druidry: Magical Spirituality for the Wild Soul*, London: Piatkus Books Ltd

Restall Orr, E. (2007) *Living With Honour: A Pagan Ethics*, O Books

Restall Orr, E. (2000) *Ritual: A Guide to Life, Love & Inspiration*, London: Thorsons

Talboys, G. K. (2006) *Way of the Druid: Rebirth of an Ancient Religion*, O Books

van der Hoeven, J. (2014) *Dancing With Nemetona: A Druid's Exploration of Sanctuary and Sacred Space*, Moon Books

van der Hoeven, J. (2013) *Zen Druidry: Living a Natural Life, with Full Awareness*, Moon Books

Internet Resources

The British Druid Order www.druidry.co.uk
The Druid Network druidnetwork.org
The Order of Bards, Ovates and Druids www.druidry.org
Down the Forest Path www.downtheforestpath.wordpress.com
Emma Restall Orr www.emmarestallorr.org

Suggested Reading

Brown, N. (2012) *Druidry and the Ancestors: Finding our Place in our History*, Moon Books

Brown, N. (2012) *Druidry and Meditation*, Moon Books

Billington, P. (2011) *The Path of Druidry: Walking the Ancient Green Way*, Llewellyn

Carr-Gomm, P. (2002) *Druid Mysteries: Ancient Wisdom for the 21st Century*, Rider

Carr-Gomm, P. (2002) *In the Grove of the Druids: The Druid Teachings of Ross Nichols*, Watkins Publishing

Green, M. J. (2005) Exploring the World of the Druids, Thames and Hudson Ltd

Hopman, E. E. (1995) *A Druid's Herbal for the Sacred Earth Year*, Inner Traditions Bear and Company

Hopman, E. E. (2008) *A Druid's Herbal of Sacred Tree Medicine*, Inner Traditions International

Hopman, E. E (2012) *Priestess of the Fire Temple: A Druid's Journey*, Llewellyn

Hopman, E. E. (2008) *Priestess of the Forest: A Druid Novel*, Llewellyn

Hopman, E. E (2010) *The Druid Isle*, Llewellyn

Hutton, R. (2011) *Blood and Mistletoe: The History of the Druids in Britain*, Yale University Press

Hutton, R. (1999) *The Triumph of the Moon: A History of Modern Pagan Witchcraft*, Oxford Paperbacks

Ly de Angeles et als (2005) *Pagan Visions for a Sustainable Future*, Llewellyn

Restall Orr, E. (2004) *Living Druidry: Magical Spirituality for the Wild Soul*, London: Piatkus Books Ltd

Restall Orr, E. (1998) *Principles of Druidry*, Thorsons

Restall Orr, E. (2000) *Ritual: A Guide to Life, Love & Inspiration*, London: Thorsons

Restall Orr, E. (1998) *Spirits of the Sacred Grove: The World of a Druid Priestess*, Llewellyn

Talboys, G. K. (2011) *The Druid Way Made Easy*, O Books

Talboys, G. K. (2006) *Way of the Druid: Rebirth of an Ancient Religion*, O Books

Treadwell, C. (2012) *A Druid's Tale*, John Hunt Publishing

van der Hoeven, J. (2014) *Dancing With Nemetona: A Druid's Exploration of Sanctuary and Sacred Space*, Moon Books

van der Hoeven, J. (2013) *Zen Druidry: Living a Natural Life, with Full Awareness*, Moon Books

Other Books by the Author

Dancing With Nemetona:
A Druid's Exploration of Sanctuary and Sacred Space

Nemetona is an ancient goddess whose song is heard deep within the earth and also deep within the human soul. She is the Lady of Sanctuary, of Sacred Groves and Sacred Spaces.

She is present within the home, our sacred groves, our rites and all the spaces that we hold dear to our hearts. She also lies within, allowing us to feel at ease wherever we are in the world through her energy of sanctuary and transformation. She holds the stillness and quiet of a perfect day; she is the stillness at the end of it, when the blackbird sings to the dusk. She is the energy of sacred space, where we can stretch out our souls and truly come alive, to be who we wish to be, filled with the magic of potential.

Rediscover this ancient goddess and dance with a Druid to the songs of Nemetona. Learn how to reconnect with this goddess in ritual, songs, chants, meditation and more.

Zen Druidry – Living a Natural Life, With Full Awareness

Taking both Zen and Druidry and embracing them into your life can be a wonderful and ongoing process of discovery, not only of the self, but also of the entire world around you. Looking at ourselves and at the natural world around us, we realise that everything is in constant change and flux – like waves on the ocean, they are all part of one thing that is made up of everything. Even after the wave has crashed upon the shore, the ocean is still there, the wave is still there – it has merely changed its form. Zen teachings and Druidry can combine to create a peaceful life path that is completely and utterly dedicated to the here and now, to the earth and her rhythms, and to the flow that is life itself.

These books are available through Moon Books, Amazon and other bookstores.

About the Author

Joanna van der Hoeven was born in Quebec, Canada. She moved to the UK in 1998, where she now lives with her husband in a small village near the coast of the North Sea.

Joanna is a former Trustee of The Druid Network. She has studied with Emma Restall Orr and the Order of Bards, Ovates and Druids. She has a BA Hons English Language and Literature degree from UCS.

She is regularly involved in charity work and working for her local community.

For more information about the author, please see her website at www.joannavanderhoeven.com.

MOON
BOOKS

Moon Books invites you to begin or deepen your encounter with Paganism, in all its rich, creative, flourishing forms.